Blogging For Beginners

Proven Strategies for Marketing Your Blog in 2019 and Making a Profit with Your Writing by Creating Multiple Streams of Passive Income

Contents

Introduction

You have probably heard much conflicting information about blogging in 2019. Some people swear it is the exploding business platform of the future, while others claim it is dead or dying. How do you know which is true? Take a moment to examine your perception and participation with blogs. Do you find them valuable? Interesting? Engaging? Relevant? Do you find tips and techniques through various forms of information shared online by real users, not companies? If you answered yes to any or all of these, then you are living proof that blogging is still alive and very relevant for 2019. And you are the perfect person to begin making a full-time income using your voice online.

You can sift through a lot of information online about how to get started blogging, but it can be hard when some of the information is designed for the hobby blog and blogger. These are people just putting out ideas and content because it is their personal outlet, not to make money. You are here because you want to do that to some extent, but you want to get paid for it. The purpose of this book is to help you get started with your blog and making money in a real and applicable way.

Get excited to learn about the basics of blogging and money making, how to get it all started, and how to share it with others. You will also learn about various ideas to help you generate income through your blog as well as how to move blogging from a part-time side-hustle to generating a full-time income.

Chapter 1: Blogging for Profit – The Basics You Need to Know

Can You Really Make Money Blogging?

So, you know what a blog is, you know that people make money doing it, and you want to get in on the action. But do you really know how it makes you money? And is it really feasible to think that a blog can make a "day-job" be sustainable income? There are a few ways a blog makes money, and it depends on what you want to talk about and how you want to approach your blogging career. The purpose of this section is just to get you thinking about some different topics, which will be explored in more detail later in the book. In addition, you will have the opportunity to take a short "quiz" to help you figure out just what "kind" of blogger you are so you can start customizing your blog and your monetization accordingly.

Below is a list of different ways many bloggers make money through their sites. Again, you will learn more about what these really are, how they work, and if they make sense for your style of blog. However, right now, you can see the many different methods used that you can pick and choose from later.

1. Cost Per Click, or CPC
2. Pay Per Click, or PPC
3. Cost Per 1,000 Impressions, or CPM
4. Private advertising space
5. Affiliate links
6. Sell online services or products such as:
   a. E-books
   b. Online workshops and courses
   c. Music, videos, and images that can be re-used in other's content
7. Content marketing
8. Memberships

Sometimes, simply creating valuable content and sharing advice is important enough that people will begin to see you as a resource and expert. You will become the name and business they associate with your industry. When they need something from your sector, you are the first stop on their purchasing journey. This can take a long time to establish. However, when you can generate followers in this manner and develop your reputation in this way, it is one of the most successful ways of building an income stream from blogging. Of course, this is best done for the Corporate or Entrepreneur blogger.

This leads into the different bloggers you may interact with and can help determine where you fall in the mix of all of this. Below is a quick introduction to some of the various types of bloggers online today:

1. *The Entrepreneur*: This person is blogging for their business. Sometimes, the blog is their business, while other times, they have another business that they are promoting through the use of their blog.
2. *The Corporate*: While blogging, Corporate is building content and a reputation for their company. Blogging may not be their full-time job, but they spend a considerable amount of their time focused on it.

3. *The Full-Time Pro*: You will see this pop up from time to time on a job board or company website, "blogger for hire." This position is brought into a company for the sole purpose of writing, monitoring, and managing their online presence, specifically their blog. This role creates content for the site, and also finds guest contributors or contributes to other blogs in an effort to raise awareness for this company's site.

4. *The Part-Time Pro*: Unlike the Entrepreneur or Full Time Pro, this person has a completely separate job. This job may influence the blog, but it is not about the business or company necessarily. This is the supplemental income-type of a blog.

5. *The Hobbyist*: Sometimes, a blog is just meant to be fun. Sure, it can turn into something more lucrative someday, but sometimes, it is enjoyable just to put things out there to share with others. Contributions are usually just a few times a week, and there is no real income generated through this content.

You may easily determine right now how you fall into these categories, or you may be swaying from one area to the next. For example, if you own a business, you could be deciding if you want to blog as part of that business, do something separate as a Part-Time Pro, or even just create a blog as a Hobbyist. If you do not own a business, you have the choice of being a Part-Time Pro, Hobbyist, or even an Entrepreneur. You can also approach your current company to ask about becoming a corporate content marketing professional as part of your role. To help you determine what the best fit is for you, take the quiz below and find out!

1. When you think about writing a blog post that is new and engaging, you feel:
   a. YAY! This is going to be awesome!
   b. I'm not sure I have the time to start and finish that project...
   c. Okay, but how is it going to make me money?

d. AH! I'm staring at a blank page and can think of nothing to write!

2. What kind of content do you like to engage with, make, or think you want to make?

    a. Your favorite things with reviews or styled images.

    b. Tips for travel such as booking suggestions and itineraries for favorite places.

    c. How-tos with detailed instructions.

    d. A piece that highlights my personality and full of personal content.

3. What ways will you publish your content or do you think will make sense for you when blogging?

    a. Through personal social sites like Facebook and Instagram to the general public.

    b. Online groups and forums.

    c. Using a service like Co-Schedule, Hootsuite, or Buffer to schedule your posts.

    d. Only to my friends and family through Facebook or a single social site.

4. What statement below feels like it fits best with your goals or ideas about blogging?

    a. My blog needs to reflect my passions. I realize that not all my ideas and passions are "money makers", but I want to find something that I love that can also generate an income stream.

    b. While money is the primary object of my blog, I want to use the influence of the blog and the money it generates to not only fuel my dreams but help others as well.

    c. I want to make money. It does not matter what the content is about; all I care about is making money. That is my inspiration.

    d. The desire to make a difference in the world through my purpose and passion are the only reasons for me putting myself out there like this.

5. The last time you went shopping you bought:

a. New high heels that were on display in the window of the fancy store you like.

b. A backpack, travel bag, or suitcase.

c. An online training, workshop or class.

d. A fresh notebook because all of your other notebooks are filled with stories, musings, and ideas. Or you bought it because you love the idea of selecting an opportunity for words of wisdom.

6. Fill in the last of this sentence, "Right now, I would rather be..."

a. Shopping for the latest styles and accessories.

b. Traveling to somewhere new and/or exciting.

c. Making money!

d. Writing! Anything and everything, just getting it out on "paper".

7. Imagine you have posted a new blog post and a few people have started leaving comments. What do you think people will say about your writing?

a. "Great find! It is so perfect. I need to buy this for my wardrobe/house/etc."

b. "What an experience! Thanks for sharing."

c. "Thank you! This was super helpful."

d. "This is the funniest thing ever!"

8. Choose the statement that best fits your personality:

a. You never know who is watching or when an opportunity arrives, so always dress your best. After all, your world is your stage!

b. You are not afraid of seeking adventure. In fact, you crave finding something new to explore near and far.

c. What you know you have to teach. When you learn something new, you want to share it with others to help them with their learning.

d. I love so many areas of life; it is hard to pick just one! When I learn something new, I want to go all in and find out more and more. I am passionate about many areas of life.

If you answered mainly "a": You are setting trends. Maybe it is not about fashion; maybe it is about the home or another trend, but you are spotting it and rocking it, and others tune in to learn from you. It is a form of "hobbyist" but can turn into a great entrepreneurial or part-time professional path.

If you answered mainly "b": You are moving and grooving, and people want to see it. You share your experiences for a number of reasons, but the primary one is that you are passionate about it. You could be doing this as part of a position, meaning you are Full-Time blogger or Part Time Professional, but you can also pursue this path as a Hobbyist.

If you answered mainly "c": You are a business blogger. You are most likely doing this as a full-time job or part of a job.

If you answered mainly "d": You are a lifestyle, hobby blogger. You may turn it into something financially supportive or maybe something part time, but most of the time, you are turning to this outlet for your passions rather than a purse.

When you are a Travel Blogger…

You are a thrill seeker and want to reflect your adventures. You live a life full of passion and excitement, or at least you want to. The idea of your blog as a way to live this lifestyle all the time or more often is attractive to you. You are looking to use it to fund your adventures or at least encourage you to do it more often.

It is likely that you search for and embrace new opportunities. You like to be flexible and free to do what you want. You also do not do well with a project that does not inspire you, no matter how much money you can make from it. This is where you could pursue your blog as a Hobbyist, rather than for income. On the other hand, you could use the monetization of your blog to fund your travels and life. To help you make money with this type of blog, consider finding brands and businesses that support your travel interests. These brands can provide affiliate links, paid advertisements, or PPC.

When you are a Trendsetting Blogger...

You are looking for the newest "hot" topic or item. You are the person that people go to in order to learn about the latest and greatest. You always are watching what people are doing and talking about and bringing it into your life in some way. This can be fashion related, or it can be about technology, design, food, or more. You are also a host of tips, tricks, and techniques on the latest new thing.

Sometimes, this pursuit can seem uncertain because you are pioneering the way and are not sure if anyone is going to follow along. This is normal for this position; trust in your ability to see what is coming and bring new light to an area that needs it. Some things will fail, but most likely you are on top of topics, ensuring your success on the upward trajectory. This is a business and profit-making blog. Sometimes, this is connected to another business, making you a Full Time or Part Time Professional. Occasionally, you will see this type of role also categorized as a corporate blogger. Consider adding affiliate links to your site for best monetization.

When you are a Lifestyle, Blogger...

You are a being with many interests. You can not really surprise those that you are close to because they know just how dynamic you really are. Sometimes, it is hard to stick to one topic for a long time because you have so many interests—it is hard to pick. This means your blog could cover a host of topics like fashion, home, beauty, cooking, travel, etc. The topics you share are often instructional and inspirational. People like to read what you have to say because it is so passionate and diverse. Most of the time, the topic in these blogs is shared amongst friends and neighbors because of the connection to their lives. This is an in-demand field because of its power to influence. This means you can find yourself successful as a Part-

Time Pro, a Full-Time Professional, or Entrepreneur. In addition, you can pursue this as pure passion being a Hobbyist. It can be a challenge if you are a Corporate blogger because this is a heavy passion project. It can also be a challenge as a Full-Time Professional if your business is not multi-faceted and you are not passionate about what they are offering to the community.

Monetization can occur in almost any way you decide, and that does not interfere with your passion presentation. Make sure your personality is not overshadowed by the advertising and affiliate links for the best success.

When you are a Business Blogger…

You are knowledgeable and experienced. You know your industry, whatever that is, and are willing to share some of what you have learned along the way. Other times, you have a new idea that you want to introduce to the industry and need a platform to present the idea and vet it for fresh perspectives. This is also a very passionate outlet for sharing messages, but often, the driver of money and profit is what motivates you more than the desire to share information. Not always, but often. Do not let this drive for income overtake your unique perspective, offerings, and voice. That is what sets your business apart from the competition, so let it shine in your blog too. Also, do not get so caught up in monetization that you miss the content. You will not make money if your blog posts are not engaging. Keep your audience and customers in mind before the money, and you will bring in both well.

Blogging in 2019: Why Do It Now

Ten years ago, blogging was a completely different "animal" than it is today. Before, it was just a simple platform for sharing ramblings or advice. Now, they are stylish, well-organized, and responsive. Algorithms have been updated to favor the blog topics. Of course, with these advances, more people are flocking to the medium, making for more competition than before. However, while there is competition, you have an amazing opportunity. Now, more than ever, people are looking for honest and real reviews, experiences, and tutorials. People are looking for real-life information more than advertisements online or websites offering information provided by the business. For example, one of the most popular features on Amazon is the filter for average reviews. People make their purchasing decision based on the reviews of other shoppers more than the description of the product and even the price.

Some advice floating around is that no one wants to read long posts, so keep your content short and sweet, or people are only watching videos, so do not waste your time writing down something you can show them. The truth is that people are interacting with the written word through blog formats more than ever, in addition to short tutorials or commentary and videos. Blogging is a viable method for making money, building a business, and following your passions. Now, also more than ever, you can find an outlet for your creativity and passion that others are also searching for. In the age where the Internet and access are with us at all times, you can offer information in a valuable and personal way. People are searching for a personal connection, and your voice may be just the thing they are looking for. In addition, incorporating various income streams help safeguard you against economic impacts like the Recession. There are just so many benefits to blogging that it makes sense to get started now. It is not too late to create an outlet and make some money doing it.

Why You Need a Niche

Once you decide that you are going to start blogging and choose what type of blogger you are going to start out as, then you need to know what you are going to write about. Yes, like a Hobbyist or Lifestyle blogger, you can cover a myriad of topics, but most of the time, you want to boil it down to something predictable and comprehensive. People are looking online to find information about something; usually, a question or problem they have and they need an answer. If they find your blog, you better work on presenting that information to them in a helpful and clear way. Rambling on will not solve their problems! Choosing a niche means you narrow down

11

your audience and tailor your content to their needs. For example, you provide fashion advice to the working mom or travel tips to the millennial. Not only do you find a small group to talk to, but you give them content they value, so they keep coming back.

Finding this niche is not always an easy task. It could be like staring at a blank page urging words to come, or you could feel like you are swimming in a sea of ideas and choosing one is like grasping a single water drop. The simple place to start is to settle on what you are passionate about. Passion is what breathes behind all successful blogs. If you love what you are writing and sharing, your readers will feel it. This keeps them connected and wanting to be a part of it. In addition, your passion motivates you to put more time into the project and can sustain your efforts for a longer period. It can take months for your blog to start making real money and focusing on a passion can help you get there. Passion also has very few limits. You can probably find a million things to talk about when it comes to something you love.

If the idea of finding or uncovering a "passion" seems daunting, begin by listing out things that you do such as hobbies or activities you participate in during your free time. Is there something that your friends and family joke about like "opening a can of worms" when someone brings the topic up around you? Was there something in school or in your earlier years that you loved learning about or doing? This could include something that you read or took a class on and still want more. Another way to look at is like you get to choose one thing you can do for the rest of your life. What would that one thing be? You may think everyone will say the same thing, but in reality, your dreams and passions may be just different enough from what is out there and still resonate with a whole group of people.

Below is a list of questions you should answer to help pinpoint a potential niche for your blog. You can use this to guide you or follow your own instincts:

1. List out all your hobbies or activities or that you wish were your hobbies.

2. List out things you enjoy doing or that you think you would enjoy doing.

3. Think about how you spend your free time or would want to spend your free time and write down what you do.

4. If you were asked for advice on a specific topic, what is one thing you could speak about with confidence and knowledge for awhile?

5. When you were a little child, what activities did you love? What was the most fun thing you remember as a child?

6. Do you take classes or workshops on something? Do you want to learn more about a specific topic? What area have you done the most training in?

It is okay if you choose something and are still unsure of the niche. Get into your blog and start putting content out there. If your niche begins to transform and move with your passion and audience, that is great! If you settle into the niche and begin to dominate the market, that is great too! No, you do not want to bounce around from topic to topic without a plan, but you are also not tied down to one niche for the rest of your life. You can let it naturally evolve with the people you are engaging and your interests.

To dominate your niche, you need to know your niche. You need to offer content that engages your niche. When you get in this sweet spot, you are now ready to bring up the interaction a notch. Maybe you do something different that has not been done before, or cover a hot topic in a new way, or even expand on something that was a popular discussion a month or so ago. Find holes in your competition's information and add a fresh spin to old topics. In addition to finding a great fit for an audience, you will also find a great fit for advertisers and businesses. As you start to partner with businesses on your site for promotion and monetization, you can make sure that the brands you bring on really do fit with your audience and they can easily see this fit through the content you are posting and the comments of the people engaging with you.

Some people choose to go through a network rather than a niche and independent blog. That is an okay method for promoting work and content; however, if you want to make a profit targeting a select group of people, having an independent blog with a clear niche is a much more lucrative approach. Niches and networks do not mix well together. A network can provide income faster than a stand-alone blog; however, your blog offers freedom of frequency, and you can pocket all the profits.

Passive Income Explained

Blogging is not a passive activity. It takes time, dedication, and effort. Sometimes, people get confused with blogging activity and the idea of "making money while you sleep". Your blog can bring money to you while you are sleeping because of the effort you put into it while you were awake. It is not something you can just set and then forget about and start making a ton of cash. This is very important to remember. With that knowledge, you can move forward and create an amazing blog that keeps bringing you new sources of income. There are a few things you can do now that can continue to bring you income long term. Below is a list of different income generators that have a great "shelf life:"

> • *Personal templates and checklists.* What are you blogging about? Are you sharing information about your financial knowledge? What tool can you develop that would be valuable to your readers to use? Think of an Excel budgeting tool or tracker. Are you writing about travel? Create a guidebook with tips for visiting different places you have been or a list for how to effectively pack a suitcase for international travel. Once you create this, make it easy for your readers to find on your blog and promote it. The more the word gets out about how awesome it is, the more people are going to buy it and continue to buy it for a long time.

• *Give dropshipping a try.* You can sell physical items on your blog that correlate with your niche but never actually hold any inventory personally. This is called dropshipping. There are various companies out there that will produce the inventory and hold it until you tell them what to ship and to where. There are many suppliers and methods you can choose from to add this feature to your site. It would be wise to set up a system for monitoring your sales and communicating with your supplier, but the front end work can be worth all the passive income on the backend.

• *Share your knowledge in more detail.* If you are an "expert" or very knowledgeable about a certain topic, the chances are that you could write for days on it and share a ton of information. Maybe you have shared a bunch of it already but keep getting requests for more on different areas. And in the digital world, you do not need to worry about selling a physical book. Create a digital e-book and sell it on your site. Set it at a reasonable price and promote it to your readers and through an auto-responder email function. Once you write the book, it is an "evergreen" product you can sell passively for years and years.

• *Promote what you use for profit.* If you are writing about a topic on your blog, it is probably because you are passionate about that area in your personal or professional life. This also means that you are probably using products related to this area in some way. You will learn more about affiliate links, but the basics are this: when you talk about a product on your blog, add a link for the reader to purchase it. When the reader buys that product from your link, you get a portion of the sales. If you are already using the products and services, it is a great "win-win".

• *Create a custom course.* This is especially helpful if you are sharing knowledge and tips already on a topic. Professional and Corporate bloggers can rock this income opportunity, develop a course on a teaching platform and sell it to your readers. You can offer an in-person course, but that can be a challenge with people not signing up in time or not enough signed up to dedicate the time to it. Instead, consider offering a pre-recorded class that readers can download or receive over a series of weeks to learn the skills. The added benefit of this passive income option is that you can charge a good amount for what you have to offer.

• *Challenge your readers to change their life*. When you see that your readers are looking to make meaningful changes in their lives, you can help them push outside of their comfort zones. Creating a fun and engaging challenge that can help your readers make real, positive changes in their lives can be valuable. This can be a pre-recorded presentation, or it could be an email series with information and accountability built into it. Once you set it up, promote it, and watch it keep making you money for years to come.

Earning money while you share your passion and knowledge with your readers is a goal, not a dream. You can make it happen with a plan and action. There are many things you can do to make that money, even more than the quick list above, but never forget that the act of blogging is not a passive process. You must still generate content that engages and reaches your readers. This takes time and effort. The things you do in support of this can bring in passive income in addition to the other income streams you develop for your site. In addition, not all forms of passive income make sense for what you have to offer to your niche audience. Make sure to choose something that is worthwhile to your readers and that you can realistically offer them. For example, a training course may be a challenge for a travel blogger but could be great for a tech blogger that can share how to get the most out of smart home features. A challenge may not fit with your readers who come to you for funny quips and fashion reviews, but it works great for a beauty blogger encouraging their readers to embrace a safer or more affordable approach to their appearance.

Take the time to think about what you think you could add to your readers and their experience with your blog in a meaningful and realistic way. Maybe you already have thought up some options to add to your site, or you are still rolling the ideas around to see what will stick with the words you are offering to readers. Whatever you decide to do, for the best passive income strategies, choose to spend your time on something that will continue to make your income well after you put it out for sale.

Success Stories: Bloggers Who Earn $10,000+ a Month

There are "real" bloggers out there making "real" money with what they have grown and created. The idea of making money through writing about your passion online is not unrealistic or out of reach. First, look at some bloggers and blogs that are making a great amount of money:

1. Huffington Post: $2,330,000/month
2. Mashable: $560,000/month
3. Perez Hilton: $450,000/month
4. Techcrunch: $400,000/month
5. Smashing Magazine: $190,000/month
6. Timothy Sykes: $150,000/month
7. Gothamist: $110,000/month
8. Tuts Plus: $110,000/month
9. Car Advice: $70,000/month
10. Venture Beat: $62,000/month

These blogs have invested time and resources into building them into the success they are today. This is possible, but you have to do the leg work as they have in order to see their level of success. On the other hand, there are "everyday bloggers" that are also making a good amount of money each month that you can learn from. The following list of people are some bloggers who make $10,000/month or more:

- Jorden Makelle
- Jeff Rose
- Natalie Bacon
- Greg Kononenko
- Allison Lindstrom
- Morgan Timm
- Lena Gott
- Ramit Sethi
- Matthew Woodward
- Pat Flynn
- Neil Patel

These people have also invested time and effort into building their blogging platform and reaching readers but in a different way. You can do this too! Below are some tips that these people have shared to help you find your success in getting started with blogging to produce an income:

1. Find the "fruit" that is hanging in a particular topic or niche. Search with popular and trending keywords and look for things that are missing. That is your opportunity.

2. Be smart about your content. Cut long posts into smaller chunks and repurpose topics that could benefit from video or infographics, for example.

3. Be clear about what the reader is going to experience throughout your post. Use headings, subheadings, snippets, call out's, images, etc., to help guide and inform your reader through your content.

4. Pay attention to what counts. The content that converts is the content you should focus on. This allows you to drive more traffic to those converting pages but also gives you a format for developing converting content again in the future.

5. Start small and grow big. This includes your reach but also your ideas. If you think something will resonate, test it out for free to gauge the response. If it is hitting the target on the small set, go all out with a paid advertisement to promote it

to more people. This approach helps you determine what is best to spend your money on and what is best to be left as a pleasant surprise for readers but did not cost you in advertising. Your posts should also be "small" in the sense that it should cover one topic and offer one solution. Be specific with the solution in one post. If there is more than one solution, turn it into a series and grow the information in multiple posts rather than one long, intense one.

6. Grow loyalty, not fans. Having a million fans on your pages is great, but only if a good amount of them are doing more than just skimming your headlines now and then. Instead, focus your attention on growing a loyal group of converting readers.

7. When you begin, offer great value for free. For example, if you are working on a course that you want to sell through your blog, offer tips on the subject for free through your blog or free downloads with great content that leads well into the topic of your course. This way, you establish a reputation as knowledgeable and helpful, and readers will know the value of your work and why you are charging for it in the future. This is also a great method for having a high price for a product or service and getting real customers to engage with it.

8. Keep a calendar and block off time to dedicate to this. You want to make sure you are consistent and in touch. Give yourself time every week to review what is relevant to your audience, come up with ideas for content, and enough time to create and edit it. You can always prepare ahead of time and set content to auto-publish on a specific day and time, but you always want to keep a pulse on your readers. This means doing your research and taking the time to make this something valuable.

Chapter 2: Starting Your Blog

Getting Started: Platforms, Hosting, Domains

Welcome to the world of setting up a blog site or platform. This can become a bit confusing because there are a variety of different options out there for you to consider, and all of the hosting sites you look at will say they are the best. This is not wrong; they are all great in one way or another, but there are some very important things you need to know at the start to help you choose the best domain, host, or platform for your money-making blog.

Remember that your blog is a site focused on writing content that is valuable to your audience and niche. You can include things like audio, images, and video, but the focus is on the written word. It is great to have a clear and active place for people to comment on your content. This way you have a connection to your readers directly and can use this interaction to form your future content. It is also how readers can learn to trust your position as a leader in your area. This does not mean you need to be a true "expert" or "leader" in an industry, but rather you are leading the conversation on the topic you presented in a personal and knowledgeable way. This is where passion plays a big part. However, since you already know this, now you need to know how to set it up and in a way that is best for making money.

There are six basic steps for starting your blog:

1. Choose a name
2. Choose a hosting site and register your blog name
3. Select a template for your blog and set it up
4. Create your content and post it to your site
5. Make sure to insert one or more ways for your content to generate money for you
6. Promote your content across the Internet

As you begin choosing the name for your blog, you will be looking at domain names as well. This is because someone may have already scooped up your great idea for a blog or website name! No sense in getting all ready to publish a new blog that does not have a domain name that matches it. This does not mean your domain name needs to match your blog name exactly, but it should be clear and obvious in the connection. If you run into a situation where your domain name is taken, try the name with a different extension. For example, if you wanted **www.blogblog.com,** but it is taken, check to see if **www.blogblog.net** or **www.blogblog.org** is available. The .com extension is the most popular, but it may not be the best for your site or content. If that still does not do it, try adding in a short word to the domain name, like **www.MyBlogBlog.com** or **www.ABlogBlog.com**. Another idea is to add dashes between the words. Spaces are not allowed in a domain name, but a well-placed dash can work wonders. To continue with the example, it would look something like **www.My-Blog-Blog.com**.

Once you determine your domain name, you are ready to get your content online. Thankfully, with all the hosting sites and platforms to choose from out there, you can choose something that you like, and that fits your budget. A host or hosting site is a place that puts all the things you will most likely need into one neat package so your users can experience a professional and functional interaction. It is necessary to have a host for your blog. You can always build yours from the ground up, or you can work with a company that has it pretty easy and simple to get going. Software or hosts or platforms for blogs are all a little different, but some of the most popular are:

1. Wordpress
2. Wix
3. Blogger
4. Tumblr
5. Medium
6. Squarespace
7. Joomla
8. Ghost
9. Weebly

Before you start slogging through all the in's and out's of each hosting site or platform, you want to make sure you choose a platform that is easy to use and has the growth you plan for your blog. This requires an opportunity for growth if you want it. If you choose a platform now because it is free or inexpensive, it could be a big pain later when you want to change. And, obviously, you want to make sure your choice is set up to allow you to make money easily!

Below is a quick Pro/Con list of the platforms mentioned above:

WordPress

Pro: Control over all parts of your site. Popular. Allows for growth. Offers extra features like forums and paid memberships. Many free templates and plug-ins. SEO friendly.

Con: Backup and security are on you. It does require some training and a learning curve.

Cost: Free up to $23/year.

Wix

Pro: Plenty of options for customization. No coding necessary. Easy to use. Set up is quick.

Con: Limited free functions. Changing a template or background is nearly impossible to do. E-commerce is limited.

Cost: Free to $25/month.

Blogger

Pro: Free. Easy to manage and utilize without a tech background. Supported by Google. Reliable and secure.

Con: Limited and basic. Cannot add new features as your blog grows. Few templates to choose from. Updates are infrequent. Google has control over your blog and can suspend or cancel it without notice.

Cost: Free.

Tumblr

Pro: Free with Tumblr subdomain. Ease of use and set up. Social media is well integrated. Offers a micro-blog option which can be beneficial for short posts like GIF's, images, and audio.

Con: Features are limited that could dampen your growth. No additional features for their various templates. Importing or backing up your blog is a challenge.

Cost: Free.

Medium

Pro: No coding or setup skills required. Easy to start. Can connect to an existing online community with like-minded interests. The focus is on writing a great blog, not on design.

Con: Very limited features. Your audience is on Medium, so if you leave or move your blog to a new host, you lose your audience. Not a customized domain name. Money making opportunities are limited.

Cost: Free.

Squarespace

Pro: Simple, professional templates. Offers other domain names with e-commerce opportunity.

Con: Limited features. Integration is limited.

Cost: Varies up to $40/month.

Joomla

Pro: Powerful to build just about any type of site. Hundreds of templates. Extensions available.

Con: Small community. Limited support. Security, updates, and backup is your responsibility.

Cost: Free to $23/month.

Ghost

Pro: Blog and writing focus. Intuitive interface. JavaScript for speed. Setup is not required.

Con: Customization with apps is a challenge. Limited options including themes. Can be complicated to install on your own.

Cost: Free to $29/month.

Weebly

Pro: Drag-and-drop usability. Quick setup. Try out services before paying for them.

Con: Features cannot be added to templates. Third-party integration is limited. Changing your blog to another site is challenging.

Cost: Free to $38/month.

Money-Making Niches: Which One's yours?

You are looking to make money, but you also want to focus on something you are interested in. In fact, the best way to choose a niche is to pick topics you enjoy and feel fulfilled by, but also create content that reaches your audience. Your targeted readers should be looking for and demanding your content. Once you find this intersection, it is time to look at how you can make a profit through monetization. If you can figure out ways to profit from that combination, you have found a great niche. Now, the level of monetization, demand, or fulfillment is up to you. You could choose something that you are completely fulfilled by but do not make a lot or any money from; this is the Hobbyist blogger. On the other hand, you could choose a niche that you know will make you a lot of money but is one you are not as passionate about; this is a Full-Time Professional or Corporate blogger. Neither of these "extremes" is bad, but it is just what is best for you.

Below is a breakdown out of different niche approaches depending on your preference: *passion, monetization, or demand.*

Passion

The old saying, "Follow your passions and success will follow," is not as easy as it sounds. In reality, your passion needs to be fueled and developed by hard work and effort. Instead of approaching this arena from a personal perspective, as in "What can this niche do for me?" consider it from the view of, "What can I offer to others?" Approaching your passion in this way is what ensures that it makes you money and brings success. Share what you know in a way that helps others with their problems, so you do not just "toot your horn".

Monetization

To determine the profitability of your niche, look to the competition. If there are many others in your niche, you have an opportunity. If you know these blogs are making money, and good money, you are in the right spot. Competition is good in blogging because everyone has a personality and perspective. Yours can be valuable too.

Demand

When you are approaching passion in a serving manner instead of the selfish way, you are creating content of value. This leads very well to demand. People want value, and that is what you have got. The more people you can help, the better the demand for your voice. As you figure out the problems of others and how your interests and experiences help them, the more successful you will become. This success is what leads to more profit opportunity.

Common Niche Themes

- Business Blogs: Marketing blogs are especially popular and have a lot of competition. Remember: this is not bad! People want help, and you can help them! Now, just because you have a voice, though, you are still going to be talking alongside some of the brightest professionals in your field. This could mean that you focus your content to a field that does not have "great" marketing skills already. The great thing about this niche is that you can offer services and products for top-dollar and sharpen your skills. On the other hand, competition is high level.

- Hobby Blogs: This is a big niche, especially on the social platform Pinterest. You can quickly and easily build a successful blog in this area when you leverage the connection to Pinterest. There is great potential for SEO, and you can easily sell products on sites like Etsy and Shopify. Unfortunately, the price of products is often lower than other niches.

- Culinary Blogs: Advertising is the biggest revenue stream for culinary blogs. Unfortunately, this means that many people need to get to your site first before it starts making money. This visitation can happen quickly if you have a strong Pinterest strategy. Social media and SEO are ripe with demand for topics on culinary trends. In addition, there is much opportunity for sponsored posts from various brands. If you can react fast on a trend, you can make a big impact. On the other hand, coming up with a great recipe with quality photos and testing can take a lot of time. Also, most people are coming to these sites for free recipes. Selling products is hard when you are giving away their demand for free.

• Fashion or Apparel Blogs: Talk about visuals! This is great for social sites like Pinterest, YouTube, and Instagram. You can monetize this easily with affiliate marketing, content that is sponsored, and through advertisements. Monetization is easy to accomplish with this type of niche. In addition, the competition is not as high level. However, the problem with a fashion blog is that it is all about you and your visual life. Also, you are not typically able to sell high-priced items.

• Investing and Finance Blogs: Money does not need to just center on people interested in the finance industry. People of all walks of life and careers are looking for ways to save money, make money, cut back on spending, increase investing, etc. It is a "hot" topic on Pinterest. Use this traffic-generator to increase visitors to your site, and then capitalize with a great SEO strategy. You can focus on just about any area of investing or finance, but the area you can make the most money and charge the most is focusing on how people can make money. The best ways to capture this is by building a big readership and then introducing how to make money. There is no shortage of people looking for this information, so you should have no problems building your readership. Just remember: people, are looking for this type of information rather seasonally, typically between November and February. Also, large businesses are pursuing this niche as well so you will be competing with companies with a lot of money invested in this arena.

• Fitness-focused Blogs: For new bloggers in this field, get on to Pinterest immediately and start driving traffic to your blog. You will quickly gain a large readership. People are looking for information and solutions to their health and wellness. The best way to make money, and the most common, is with affiliate links. If you have it already or plan on it, you can develop your products to solve your reader's problems, and this is a great money-making approach. The great thing about this niche is the variety of ways you can generate revenue. The challenge, however, is that there is much competition in this niche and it is also a seasonal group, typically peaking in January.

• Lifestyle Blogs: This tilting can be misleading. This type of approach is really a multiple niche approach. The attraction is that you do not have to narrow down what interest you are going to focus on; however, you do still need to select topics that will drive readership. Pinterest is the popular social site for these blogs, and the users want visually engaging "hot" topics. In addition, the successful blogs in this arena are targeting a demographic. They are selecting topics to talk about that the majority of people in that "group" are going to be interested in. For example, mom lifestyle bloggers cover topics like caring for a newborn, the best way to travel with toddlers, how to feed a family on a budget, etc. This type of approach allows you to switch up your content based on what is trending and you will probably never get bored or burnt out because you can always change what you are working on. This format also opens the door for many diverse revenue opportunities. But on the other hand, spreading out your content across topics means you spread out your impact on SEO. In addition, targeting just a demographic and not a specific area means that your readers are coming for a variety of answers to their questions. It can be a challenge to develop a strong content marketing strategy when your readership is so diverse.

• Travel Blogs: Travel blogs are not just about sharing awesome pictures of places you have traveled, although it can be a part of it. Instead, a successful travel blog highlights interesting places that a certain group of people would be interested in visiting. The content is meant to inspire this audience to do something adventurous, too, even if it is not to travel to the place you blogged about. Drive traffic to this type of blog through various social sites, including Pinterest. You also do not need to just talk about places to visit on this platform; instead, think about offering advice about how to make money while traveling or different hacks for the best travel experiences. You can also make money from readers signing up for credit cards that target travelers. Keep in mind, however, that most successful blogs do include your personal travels. This means you must be willing to travel a lot for a long time. This can mean spending a lot of money up front before your blog becomes successful. In addition, the money readers are spending is on their travel plans. This limits your opportunity to generate money directly from them.

Know Your Enemy (aka Competitors)

Just about every great coach in the history of coaching knows that to aide your success in the game, you need to know whom you are competing against. This allows them to develop specific strategies to help them win when they get on the field. There are a million excuses not to do this; including not wanting to "stalk" someone or the idea is so great that there is no need to see what others are doing, or there is no time to look at the competition. The reality is that sooner or later, all money makers need to lift their head up from their work and look at what is happening around them. The most successful do this early before making many unnecessary mistakes. Knowing your competition, or your "enemy", gives you a great picture of where you sit in relation to the rest of the market and also offers the opportunity to develop new and valuable ideas for your readers.

It can be overwhelming to start getting to know your competition. The best place to start is through Google. If you have a niche or topic or product you want to blog about, look it up on Google. Try different keywords associated with it. If you know the question or problem you want to solve, type it into Google and see what answers are offered already. Also, look on the App store and other marketplaces to see if there is some sort of product or service that solves the problem already. Make sure you look at the two different kinds of competition while doing your research. The two different kinds of competition are direct competition, or those offering solutions to the same problem, and the indirect competition. Indirect competition is those who offer something very different but to your target audience or they offer the same type of solution but to a different group of people. The value of knowing your indirect competition is how a person will find a solution to their problem, even if the messaging is not made for them. When you find this out, you can now find a way to offer a unique solution meant just for them.

To keep track of your information, create a competition spreadsheet. Compile all the information about the competition including the branding, target audience, and products offered. If possible, try their products. Engage with their content. If you are struggling with or cannot experience all the competition has to offer, see if you can read reviews and customer experiences. To help you format your spreadsheet, consider the following information:

1. *Identification*. Make a column for the name of the competition, the URL, and if you consider them to be direct or indirect.

2. *Summary*: write one or two sentences about what you discovered in your research. This can include the values, target audience, product offerings, personality, etc. Anything that stands out to you about the competition can be mentioned here.

3. *Advantages*: What is this competitor doing that is awesome? What things are they offering that you would also want to offer?

4. *Challenges*: Find areas that your competition is missing or failing at, and read reviews and forums to find areas of opportunity.

5. *Money makers*: How is your competition making money that you can easily see?

6. *Numerical data*: List how many people follow the competition on various social sites, their website, etc. How many downloads does their app or other products get per month? The information does not have to be super accurate, but it should be reflective of your impression. It may make sense to offer a separate sub-column for each data set. You can also include the average or range of prices if the competition is offering products or services for sale.

Once you compile all this data, look at it from a big-picture view. Do not look at each competitor right now, but instead, see if you can identify a theme or major hole. You can also notice if something is working across the competition. For example, are all the competitors offering a similar product or solution? Are they all reaching the audience through a strong presence on a social media site? You want to look for what the group is doing that is working and what is still being "left on the table". Once you get the "big picture", you can move to look at each one individually and begin developing a strategy.

Now that you have all the information, you can figure out what you are going to do on your blog so that it is different from your competition as well as knowing the problems to solve. In this strategy, you are also going to begin to outline the way you plan on bringing this to your audience. This is one of the most important steps in blogging for profit. This is essential for you to succeed and thrive. It is how you offer value to your customer time and time again. Do *not* skip this step.

Integrating Social Media

It should be no surprise that social media is the best method for getting people to learn about your blog and content, but how do you effectively share this information across various sites? And which sites should you focus on for the best results? And how often should you post to them? There is so much information surrounding this topic alone, but the following information is designed to introduce you to the wide world of social media and what you can do to get your blog out there. First, learn about cross promoting. It can be as simple as just sharing the same message on a variety of platforms, but remember that you do need to make some adjustments for the audience. You cannot just copy and paste.

One of the reasons you need to change up your post from one site to the other is because there is a different audience on each site. They go to that social platform for different reasons. For example, a person may go to Pinterest to see images and find links connected to a topic they are interested in, typically a DIY topic. They do not go on LinkedIn to find a tutorial on how to bake the best banana bread or how to refinish a mid-century modern chair. They visit LinkedIn to learn more information about their career in human resources and find new candidates for an open position. Also, each platform has its post preferences and restrictions. For example, you may have a great short article you share in a post on Facebook, but Twitter makes you cut it down to no more than 140 characters. Below is a breakdown of some information you should know for a few popular social media sites you will want to consider using for blog post promotion:

1. Facebook
- "Share" and "Like" content
- Easy place for promoting blog posts in a group, page, or personal profile
- Posts can be up to 10,000 characters; however, the first 480 characters are the only ones visible in the feed
- Long posts are not as engaging. Try to keep it to 50 characters or less
- Add images for the best response
- When you upload an image with a post, it is stored in a photo album. This allows followers to be able to view your images separately from your posts
- Hashtags do not work extremely well on Facebook, but they do help it become more searchable
- Ask readers to comment and share on your posts with personal messages
- Most frequented times for Facebook are 1-4PM and 6-10PM and all day Saturday and Sunday
- Try to post once a day
- Share posts on your profile, page, and groups, but vary when you share it and change the message in the text for each share

2. Twitter

- "Tweets" and "Re-Tweets"
- Limited text message no more than 140 characters
- Images are now allowed and do help increase re-tweets
- Adding links to tweets is also good for increasing re-tweets
- Always have more than four hashtags in a post to increase the searchability of the content and increase reactions to the content
- To increase results, add a call-to-action
- Most frequented times for Twitter are 8-10AM, 11AM-1PM, and 4-7PM during the week
- The lifespan of content is eighteen minutes; therefore, you must share blog promotion more than once and on multiple days and different times

3. LinkedIn

- "Post" and "Like"
- Post on group pages, showcase pages, company pages, and in your profile
- Ability to share the post directly through LinkedIn via SlideShare or LinkedIn Plus
- Posts can have up to 600 characters, but only the first 150 are visible in feeds
- Include links and images for the best reactions
- A professional setting that still values engaging and personal content, especially if it asks for readers to interact with the content
- Curate content to appear as a "how-to" for the most opportunity for shares, comments, likes, and post views
- Most frequented times for LinkedIn are 8-10AM and 4-6PM
- Post about once a week
- For content being reshared, change the text a little bit and repost on a different day and time for the best reach

4. Pinterest

- "Pin"
- Images are the most important; the description is only intended to highlight what the post covers
- Pin descriptions can be up to 500 characters, but to get the most activity, keep it between 150 and 300 characters
- Put hashtags in the description to increase searchability
- In the description, add a link to the post and a call-to-action to boost interactions
- Most frequented times for Pinterest are 12-2PM and 7-10PM and all day Saturday and Sunday
- Post the main image the first day of a new blog post and then post additional images spread out throughout the next few weeks after the blog was posted
- Post a few times during the week until all the images are shared
- Instagram
- "Show" and "like"
- Like Pinterest, it is all about the image, but the lifespan is shorter, typically only a few hours
- The image is a square and is 1080 X 1080 pixels
- Captions for images can be up to 2,200 characters, but only the first three lines are visible in the feed, which is typically about 150 characters
- Captions can be solely hashtags because they are so important to the promotion of the post
- The keywords in the blog post make great hashtag options
- Up to 30 hashtags
- Links in captions are not clickable, but it is good practice to include the URL to direct users to your post or blog
- Most frequented times on Instagram are midday and evening Monday through Friday

- Share the main image of your blog on the first day and then share the other images over the following days up to a few weeks after

There are a few ways you can make sharing content across platforms easier for you, especially if you use WordPress. WordPress offers the option of adding a plug-in into your blog site called "Publicize". When you add this to your blog, and you publish a new blog post, you can easily share the content across all the social platforms you set up in the plug-in. It formats the post to best fit with the social media site for you. If you upgrade to a Professional or Premium plan, you can also re-share already published content seamlessly and schedule the social promotion for a certain time. When you tell WordPress to share content through social networks automatically, you will need to log into your social sites when promoted and give them permission to work with your WordPress site. After you set it up, all the work is done for you.

Blogging Trends in 2019

The beginning of 2019 has already revealed telling information about the future of blogging for this year and even beyond. Below are the trends to look forward to in 2019:

1. Over half of the world's population engages online in some way, and the number is expected to grow.
2. Reading information through blog posts is still steady with more than half the people online reading blogs.
3. Most online interaction, including blog engagement, occurs on a mobile device. More than half of online users engage with content primarily through mobile and spend about 3.5 hours on their mobile phone each day.
4. Most blogs are written in English, on average about 70%, and will continue to be so.
5. Brands are beginning to blog more. Currently, about 55% of all brands blog as a primary marketing strategy and blogging will increase in importance over time.

6. Trust is the focus of blogs, promoting the "truth" rather than the "fake news" on social platforms. Posts will look to build and maintain trust with readers.

7. The story is another important focus of blog posts. People want to hear more personal stories.

8. A video is in demand. More than 85% of traffic searching for information will engage with video in the future.

9. Live video is increasing in popularity and influence others to purchase admissions to an event similar in nature to the live video. Paying to watch a live stream is also an emerging trend.

10. Short content is engaging and giving rise to micro-blogs, sort videos, and simple graphics.

11. Longer posts are still relevant but need to be mixed in with shorter content. Google continues to favor longer content in SEO.

12. Visual content is necessary. Visuals in content all the time is already done by more than 55% of marketers today. In addition, almost 90% of marketers are already using blogs, and they have more than one image in every post. Visuals are expected to grow in importance through the year and about a quarter of all marketers plan to spend more than a quarter of their budget on this alone.

13. Content needs to be interactive to increase engagement. This includes features like quizzes, infographics, and surveys.

14. Content needs to be personalized and relevant to the reader. This is a continuing trend that is unlikely to fade in the long-term future.

15. Partnering with brands and various brands coming together will grow throughout the year.

16. Voice search is increasing in popularity, and capitalizing on this, titles posed as questions will be more important.

17. Visual search is increasing in popularity. Find ways to make your images searchable, such as with embedded links.

18. The focus of blogs is shifted from Millennials to Gen Z, the upcoming "future" generation.

19. A connection is critical. This means having your social accounts all connected to your blog but also the authentic voice you use to connect with your audience. A transparent voice that provides quality content regularly is going to remain in demand.

20. Services for sale are going to increase as partnerships decline. This includes selling workshops, courses, books, etc., to develop a steady revenue stream. However, as mentioned above, the content for sale needs to provide quality to the reader and user.

Chapter 3: Marketing Your Blog

Blog Traffic: The Whys and Hows

When you set out to create a meaningful and profitable blog, you are going to invest a lot of time into it. What you want to know is that this effort is going to be worth it. While there is no guarantee, there are things you can do to help determine if your work is going to bring in the people you need to make the money you want. Bringing people to your blog is the best way to generate revenue. After all, if no one reads your words, no one will pay you for it. So a great measurement for the success of your blog is to monitor how many people visit it. This is called "traffic". The minute you set up your blog, you should be tracking what is coming to it and track it often. One of the benefits of doing this is that you can curate your content to your readers and not waste time on topics they are not engaging with.

You can use analytics tools to help monitor the traffic and how your readers are engaging with your content. These analytical tools identify what posts readers are spending time on and who they are. The analytics also show where on your website your readers are clicking. Using this information, you can spend time on a strategy that is informed. One of the most popular ways to track your blog's traffic and review the analytics is with Google Analytics. Many hosting sites offer their own built-in analytics, but those that do not generally offer a plug-in for Google Analytics. Even if a platform offers its own analytics, you should consider adding in Google Analytics by using the website for it. This is primarily because Google is the monopoly in SEO, so it only makes sense to get their information to improve your blog's performance. In addition, if Google does not recognize your blog, it is going to have a very hard time showing up in front of anyone you are trying to reach.

If you are not sure about how to add Google Analytics to your platform, get onto Google and type in, "How to set up Google Analytics on *insert your platform here. *" Once you get it set up, do not worry if it is a little confusing or intimidating. To begin, start with small checks and balances. Measure a few things just to get the hang of the tool. Once you figure out how the tool works, you are ready to look at the big picture of your blog.

Another important factor to consider is the pages for your blog. Your blog should and probably will naturally end up with more than one page. You will probably start organizing content into different pages like an "About Me" or "Contact" page. You may also chunk up your blog content into different headers and have different kinds of posts that appear on different pages. For example, Lifestyle Bloggers may want to put cooking tips and recipes on one page while DIY tutorials for the home go on another. When you have multiple pages, it is easier for your readers to find your information quickly, but you also need to make sure your analytics are set up to handle this. With Google Analytics, it is easy. This report in Google Analytics is called "All Pages".

The steps to generate this report in Google Analytics are as follows:

1. Open Google Analytics and log in
2. Identify the section "Behavior" located in the menu on the left side
3. Click on "Site Content"

4. From the options, select "All Pages" to generate the report

Once the report is created, the information will be scattered all around for your pages. You are going to want to filter and move the information around to figure it out. For example, you may not want to gauge the success of your blog on the traffic heading to your "Contact" page. This means you will want to remove this from the results you are seeing. You can remove any page from the report that does not directly relate to your blog. For example, if you have a "Products" page, you can filter them out in relation to the performance of your blog. You can always bring that information back in at a later date if you want to. To filter, the first thing you need to do is determine your blog post URLs. For example, your posts probably have a URL like **www.website.com/blog/post#1**, etc. Every time you create a blog post, "/blog/" is used in the URL. That is what you will use to filter your report by typing it into the "Search" field of the report.

The process of filtering your results is rather simple. You enter the common path or word into your search field and then click on the magnifying glass icon to perform the search. This will then trim down the report to show you data only on the pages that contain that field in the URL. When the report adjusts to your new parameters, the blog posts will be listed out under a nice graph and various metrics listed out for each post.

The metrics in the report are important to understand. Below is a breakdown of what each item means:

1. The first field is the URL for a particular blog post. There is a small square icon in the bottom right corner of the box. This opens the content of the analysis in a new window if you click on it.
2. The second box shows "Pageviews". This tells you how many people have looked at the page during the time frame you told the report to run. For example, if you wanted to see just one day's performance, you can narrow down the

report, or you can look at it for the week, month, quarter, or even year.

3. The following column indicates how many people visited the blog post specifically during that same time frame.

4. The average time spent on the page is valuable information. It tells you how long you captured the attention of a reader. Do not get too hung up on this information though. Google can easily misjudge it, especially if you have a high bounce rate.

5. "Entrances" refers to a reader that arrives at your blog post directly. From there, they can engage with your site in another way, like reading another post or visiting another page. This does not refer to a reader that came to your site from somewhere else and then engaged with your blog post.

6. "Bounce Rate", as mentioned earlier in this list, refers to the percentage of readers who entered your site through your blog post directly and then left after engaging in it. These readers do not go to another page or another part of your site after interacting with your specific blog post.

7. "% Exit" is a similar metric, but this refers to the people that came to your blog post from other areas or engaged differently before leaving after engaging with this specific post.

You can use this information to look at the performance of just one blog over a span of time or you can compare your blogs to find certain topics or information that stands out. While this information is very important, you need to recognize that it is not always perfect and accurate. There are always little factors that can throw off your metrics or weirdly skew your data. This means you cannot count on it 100%, but it is the best tool to really gauge what people are doing on your blog.

Now that you understand the information in the "All Pages" report, you need to know how to interpret it. What numbers are "good" and what performance indicators show it is "bad"? This may not be the best way to approach it since all blogs and traffic are different and change drastically over time, but you can start to determine the following:

1. What is the most popular post or posts? Why do you think people liked these specifically? Check comments or contacts you got based on the post to try to put your finger on why your audience engaged with these the most. It could also be the length of the post that was attractive, the topic was trending, it was shared a lot on social media, or it was shared at a specific time. See if you can find something that stands out, especially if you are looking at a couple of popular posts. What is common about the two of them that you think made them more popular than the rest?

2. How can you use this information to develop a content strategy around these successful traits? If you see that your most popular posts are ones that have a short video clip and are about 500 words, can you replicate this format more often? Or were your posts shared by readers on social media after you posted on Facebook at 4 PM on a Wednesday? Can you make sure your promotion strategy includes posting at this time more often in the future?

3. In addition, you can play with your posts that are successful by adjusting or updating them in some way. This can potentially get more life from the post and show you valuable information about what your audience is interested in. For example, if a popular post is already successful, what if you added more information to it or an integrative feature, like a survey or quiz? Can you see an increase in activity again or do your readers move on?

4. Look at the length of time between your popular posts. Is there a certain amount of time between the two that you could replicate? If you increased the number of posts in a certain time frame, which means you post more frequently, do you increase traffic to your blog? If you find a "sweet

spot" for frequency, can you keep up that frequency long term? To determine this, sit down and look at your calendar. Be realistic or even overestimate how much time it will take for you to create a post. Can you do this every week? There will be more information on this later; however, it is good to start considering it now.

Beginning to understand your blog's traffic and what it means to your future strategy is vital to your growth and success. This introduction is just to "get your feet wet"; however, you can begin to formulate your approach to understanding the performance of your blog and how you plan on using your metrics to reach your audience better.

Social Media Is Your (Marketing) Friend

You want your blog to generate traffic. This means you want to use social media to your advantage. People congregate on sites like Facebook and Twitter more than any other place on the Internet. When they are looking for information, one of the first places they start is through a social media outlet. It is also where these people share their opinions and experiences openly. The people you want to reach are probably on one or more of these sites regularly. This means it is an ideal location to launch a marketing strategy. Instead of hoping that people eventually find your blog, you can design advertisements and strategy to connect with your audience.

To help you in general when using social media for promotion, consider the following tips that can be applied to just about any form of social media:

> 1. Always add a link to your posts. Get in the habit of always linking people back to your blog, even if your post is not about a recent blog post. This leads people from your quipping posts to your content-rich blog topics.
> 2. On your blog are social buttons linking to your various social media pages. At least have a link to Facebook. Add other social media platforms that you use regularly. This

leads people to follow you through social media and not just through your blog.

3. Enable others to share your blogs on social media. Most platforms have an easy feature you can add to your blog site to promote sharing of your content across a variety of social platforms.

4. Include a clickable link in your blog post to your social media. In addition, if you have a video on YouTube that you want your readers to engage with, embed the video directly into your post, right in the middle, so they can easily see it when they load your blog post.

The last suggestion brings up a good topic to review briefly; using video in your blog posts. It is a growing medium and influencer. Many people still discredit YouTube as a social media site, but it really does fall into this category. In general, because of its ability to share visual information with anyone, it is one of the most popular social media sites. Often, the majority of the video you find on other sites is cut from YouTube or can be found in a longer form on YouTube. In addition to embedding video in your blog posts, you can embed your video in a Facebook post easily. The platforms work nicely together, and the process is pretty seamless. It is a valuable tool that can be easily maximized and provides evergreen content.

Taking the time to develop your content marketing strategy through social media is worth the time and effort. You have to compete with all the other information out there, and having a strong plan on how you will do it will help you stand out from the crowd. You can also boost your impact on different platforms that already have a huge audience with constant views. Below are suggestions on how to plan an effective strategy for social media and your blog:

1. *Offer a teaser and boost it.* On Facebook, you can hint about what your upcoming blog is going to be about. Once you create the post, you then pay to boost it to a wider audience. This option allows you to pay for the engagement you get but only up to the dollar amount you are prepared to

spend and for the length of time you want it to run for. Your boosted post can include anything from words to a video. Develop anything that you think will attract the attention of your audience and get them wanting your upcoming blog post.

2. *When you post a video on YouTube, add your blog's homepage link in the description of the video.* If your video is related to your blog post directly, add a link in the video and a recorded call-to-action asking people to go there.

3. *Create cross-links on different platforms.* For whatever reason, people seem to hesitate about cross-linking content. It may be from past algorithms in Google, but in reality, Google has never cared about cross-linking as long as it is above board and the content is pertinent to one another. You can also bring people from one platform to the next to learn more about a certain subject or expand information on a topic.

4. *Create fresh content daily on Twitter and even Facebook.* The more often you post, the more hype you can generate. Of course, the content needs to be valuable, but also short. If you can keep posts fun and easy to engage with, people are more likely to enjoy them. Instead of posting a long post on Facebook, for example, consider chunking up the information into little bites that you can share over a few days.

5. Now and then, offer a giveaway. This attracts people to your blog and your social accounts. Most social media users like to get something for free when they read or engage with your material. The main objective of this strategy should be to offer quality content, but the secondary objective should be to show that you appreciate their readership and loyalty. Most of the time, the free item you choose to giveaway does not need to be elaborate or expensive. Offering an eBook or something digital like a checklist of some sort can be just as valuable to your readers as something physical.

6. *Do not discount less-popular social media sites in your strategy.* Using social media for marketing does not mean you are exempt from the social part of it. People go to social media for more personal interaction, not to engage with business marketing messages. This means you need to show people the personal side of your money-making blog, like you doing things, your family, adventures you have been on, etc. This can be done well through the less popular social media accounts for marketing, such as Instagram. The influence of Instagram as a marketing platform is evolving, but it is still not the most commonly used platform. To capitalize on this platform for your blog posts and connect to your audience, consider adding images of personal pictures related to your blog and your life. For example, if you are a food blogger, post pictures of the great food you have made or eaten, and also the not-so-great experiences or attempts. Show people you "polished" and present something amazing, but also a picture of your kitchen after a photo shoot and the mountain of dishes and things needing to be cleaned up. This approach helps show readers what your company is all about and establishes a stronger sense of connection that other platforms may not be the best for.

Pinterest Marketing in More Detail

If you noticed earlier in this book the mention of different types of blogs that benefit from promotion on Pinterest, you will probably realize how important it is to use it to your advantage for just about any type of blog you are creating. To help you start thinking about a strong Pinterest marketing strategy, consider the following for 2019:

1. *Be consistent and regular.* Like other sites, make sure you put out valuable content regularly. To help you stay on a regular schedule, consider using a service like Tailwind. This way you avoid feat-and-famine pinning and can keep your followers happy and content.

2. *Do not "repin" content to boost it in Pinterest again.* Instead, repost information from your blog again, so it is a fresh pin. Fresh and new content is favored in Pinterest in 2019, so this is the best strategy to get your content out there again without having to come up with new content over and over again.

3. *One source, many pins.* One blog can generate many fresh pinning opportunities. Make sure, with each pin, that is has a unique description. This is best for optimizing SEO and the Smart Feed algorithm on Pinterest. You can also change the landing image of an older post and create a new pin to that source. This helps reinvigorate the content without having to rewrite information.

4. *Get seasonal content out in advance.* People use Pinterest to get ideas about upcoming events, such as holidays or times of the year. For example, people start thinking about decorating for fall and back to school in late July. This means you should be getting your seasonal content up about 45 days before the holiday or event. You can create new pins for content you have already created or generate new content in advance for fresh traffic.

5. *Do not neglect your boards.* The name you choose for your boards is searchable. This means you should be choosing names that have keywords in them and a strong SEO. Also, sections on Pinterest will probably become more important in the future for searches so add a section if it is relevant to your boards.

6. *The people you follow and that follow you are important.* It is good to follow people that offer engaging content that is relevant to your blog and your audience. In addition, make sure to encourage people not just to follow you on Pinterest, but to repin your content and add valuable contributions to the site. The more engagement you get on this site, the better. It is not always about the numbers.

7. *Make your posts pinnable.* Make it simple and obvious that your readers can and should pin your content on Pinterest for you. Anyone who engages with your blog post should know that you are active on Pinterest, what images you are encouraged to pin, and how to do it easily. You can even guide them in what to say when they pin your content!

8. *Link your other social media accounts to Pinterest.* There are other visually-centered social media platforms out there, such as Instagram and even YouTube. Now you can connect them and easily share content from one to the other. And you do not need to be the one sharing it! Linking the accounts makes it easier for your audience to pin from another social site onto Pinterest. This boosts your engagement and increases your impressions and visibility. In addition, it opens up more reach for your audience and shows your readers that you are in more places for them to engage with. If they thought you were only posting a video on YouTube, but then learn you are on Pinterest, you can get them to engage more through Pinterest too. And it can work the other way around! People from Pinterest can then be exposed to your blog, Instagram, Etsy, LinkedIn, etc.

Leads and Lists: How They Work

To begin, you need to know a few things, like what exactly is a "lead", "lead generation", and "mailing list". For some of you, this may sound intuitive. For others, you may have no idea what in the world those are referring to, and even for others, you may think you know what they mean, but as you read through the definitions, you may become surprised at what you learn. Here are some short descriptions to help you before diving into the information further:

- *Leads*: Potential readers or "buyers". These people have shown an interest in some area of your blog or online presence and have willingly shared contact information with you so you can communicate more directly with them.

- *Lead Generation*: Opportunity for potential "buyers or "engagers" to share their contact information with you when they express interest in your blog or presence online. This is how you get people to give you more direct contact methods for future communication.

- *Mailing List*: The compilation of all the contact information leads have shared with you. This is how you organize the information they have shared with you and how you can contact them directly in the future more easily than trying to find a form or document with information written on it. Think of a spreadsheet with names, phone numbers, email addresses, etc. You can add information on here about how they interacted or showed interest in your online content so you can easily tailor messages to them.

Now that you know what they are, how do they really add value to your blog and making money? Here is a quick breakdown of that information for each one:

- *Leads*: People are not responsive to the "cold call". They do not want to talk with someone on the phone or in person unless they know it is valuable. However, online is another story. People are willing to engage with others online because it is less "risky". Because more people are willing to connect online, you can reach more people and people that are often hard to "catch" in person. Bringing more people to your site means more engagement. More engagement means more opportunity to make money through PPC, etc. In addition, more traffic to your blog means more opportunity for partnerships, etc.

- *Lead Generation*: Generating opportunity for leads and potential loyal readers are how you have new people to talk to. It is a fresh perspective and allows a new group of people to buy your book or sign up with the online course you created. It is how you bring people to your blog and interact with your posts. You can employ very strategic targeting methods to get the "right" types of leads for your blog instead of just putting out a message somewhere online in the hope of reaching the best people.

• *Mailing List*: There is no point in gathering all these potential readers and loyal followers if you do not talk with them. It is also not wise to gather all this information and not organize it in an easy-to-use manner. When you create a mailing list, you improve the way you can reach and communicate with those that are interested in what you have to say. This improves the quality of what you have to offer and whom you are offering it to.

Now that you know how important leads, lead generation, and mailing lists are for your social media strategy, here are several methods for generating these leads for your blog traffic and money-making success:

1. **If you want to be really savvy, create some content that is not readily available to just any visitor.** This is called "gated" content. Think of it like being hidden on your blog behind an invisible, electronic gate. Only the people with the "key" can get in to see it. The "key" in this instance is a special link or password. If they think the information you are offering to share is valuable and important enough to them, they are going to share their information with you to get access to it. The price of "admissions" is typically his or her name and basic contact information, like an email address. You can also lead people to a landing page that instructs them to put in his or her information to get access. Those that are only mildly interested will leave, but those that are still curious will exchange their information to get "in". The people willing to put in their information are the leads worth following up with. To turn your social media followers into blog engagers can be as simple as offering gated content to them. This content can be just about

anything, and you should try out a few different options to see what people respond to the most.

2. **Challenge your followers with a contest.** Make sure the prize for completing the contest is something your followers are interested in and valuable to those that have the best potential of becoming your loyal readers. This is important because people will not engage in your contest if they do not see value in the prize at the end, but it is most valuable to the people who will follow your blog loyally (and even buy your products in the future—if you decide to sell something). Remember: your contest needs to target your ideal reader. If you gather a whole bunch of leads and information, but it is not useful, it can feel like a waste of time. Instead, take some time to figure out the best reward for the people you want to stick around. Good examples of prizes include a free upgrade, a sample of a product, or access to an online workshop or training for free. These are things that you already offer that people who are most valuable to your blog would be interested in already. You can have people "enter" the challenge a few different ways; by following, liking, sharing, retweeting, tagging a specific post, or by clicking on a certain link leading to an attractive landing page. Having someone follow, like, share, etc., on social media is simple and effective. The challenge, however, is that people are then only sharing publicly available information. Also, if you do this a lot, Facebook especially, will tag your posts as spam and decrease your distribution. Asking your followers to take an extra step to go to a landing page means fewer people participating, but you can get more information, especially if you guide them to a "contest entry form" where they have to share lead information.

3. **Use the advertising options on various social media sites.** Especially being new to blogging and capturing leads, take advantage of the tools set up to help you. Yes, eventually you will learn different tips and tricks that are

more advanced, but this is still one of the best methods for gathering quality leads for your mailing list. This is probably one of the best and easiest ways to target a clear group of people effectively. Facebook is an excellent platform for this, but you can also do this effectively through LinkedIn and Instagram.

4. Offer an online live video, webinar, or hangout to generate more valuable leads. Webinars are one of the most valuable options to offer; however, you can leverage other options as well to bring people together and gather contact information. You can combine this tip with the idea of "gated" content, making people enter their contact information before they can access the video or hangout, or open the content to everyone but use the event to gather leads by encouraging participation (comments and other forms of engagement during the webinar or live video) with the reward of an attractive prize to the most engaged or by leading people to another spot on your blog for them to get a discount or more details about a contest you are running.

If these ideas seem overwhelming or intimidating, just make sure you have a place on every page of your blog for people to sign up for a "newsletter" or "special updates" from you. This way, when you post a new blog or want to share information with them, they can be in the loop. Having a pop-up on your site is good, or you can just have a place on each page with a button asking them to "stay connected" with you. This is not the most proactive way, but it is a simple and good approach to make sure you are asking people to stay loyal to your information and solutions.

SEO in 2019: Dos and Don'ts

SEO is not what it used to be. You can no longer easily spam the Internet and trick your way into the top ranks of search engines. Yes, there is still "spamdexing". This means manipulating indexes or search engine algorithms to increase SEO. Sometimes, this means link building or stringing a whole bunch of unrelated phrases together to rank higher. The risk of doing something like this is that Google will flag your blog and penalize for inappropriate processes. One of the processes Google has put in place is called Google Penguin. This algorithm is designed specifically to find people trying to manipulate the guidelines set forth by the search engine. This is great for users, but not great for those wanting to get good SEO ranking quickly by non-valuable means. This development now forces you to be a bit more strategic about your methods, which in the long run is great for your blog and the money you can make.

"SEO" is an acronym for "Search Engine Optimization". The "better" your SEO, the higher on the search engine list you get. Over time and experience, the process for determining SEO has improved, but it has always been present. In order to generate "good" SEO, you need to do certain things and avoid others. Below is a breakdown of some of the most important "dos" and "don'ts" of SEO for your blog:

The "Dos":

> 1. *Evaluate how your blog is performing with the help of analytical tools, such as Google Analytics.* This was introduced earlier and is so important that it bears repeating. Part of this process is making sure you research keywords and choose options that are relevant, popular, but not oversaturated. As you continue to read on, notice that keywords and the importance of choosing these wisely pop up time and time again.
>
> 2. *Use descriptive text to your advantage.* This also includes using keywords wisely. Especially when you are describing your blog, make sure those 55 words are well chosen. The main text for your blog description is called "Meta text" and is what you are using to attract your readers. The "tags" you choose are snippets of text that add more detail to "what" your blog is all about. Your tags need to be clear and relevant. Precision and specificity are critical. Each tag needs

to be unique, and the keywords should not be drawn out and lengthy.

3. *Insert internal links often.* You can add links in your description to help improve your SEO. Link keywords that are connected to your blog and content-wise, but choose only one internal link with a good quality keyword. If you get wild and put many internal links in a single post, you will destroy your SEO. Google considers multiple links that lead to the same place as spam and will penalize you for it.

4. *Images not only visually support your content, but also help your SEO.* Any graphics, charts, or images you put in it boost the quality of your content. While Google does not directly "see" the images in your post, it does "read" the links and tags attached to the images. Images should also have unique keywords associated with it, also revealing the quality of your post to Google. In addition, while putting "long-tail" keywords in your general blog description, you can add them to your images without penalty.

5. *Choose content that users can engage with easily.* This is also called "user-friendly" content. If you say your blog and posts will deliver something, make sure it does just that. Make sure that your visitors have a positive experience, and try to get them to stay on your site for a while by creating an easy-to-use blog site and valuable content. If they stay for a while and look around, your bounce rate lowers and your SEO increases. On the other hand, not delivering what you say you will or offering little to no value means a higher bounce rate of visitors and thereby lowering your SEO.

6. *Do not forget the importance of mobile.* A large majority of people engage with blogs and online content through a mobile device. If you are not set up to accommodate mobile viewing, you are going to get a hit to your SEO in favor of those that can deliver a good mobile experience.

7. *Use a map for your blog, even if it is just a couple of pages.* Google does not like a site that does not have an

attached site map. If you are using a host and template, most likely, this is already included for you. If you are breaking out and designing your own, make sure to include one on there for your SEO alone.

The "Don'ts":

1. *Copy content directly from another website.* It is very easy for SEO algorithms to identify content that is not fresh and that has been copied and pasted in another place. If it is done too blatantly or you do this often, your SEO will be extremely low.

2. *You have an external link overload.* Having too many links out from your blog is spamming, and Google will flag it fast. In addition, if your viewers do not find the links you are sharing relevant or functional, your bounce rate will increase, also lowering your SEO. Instead, stick to internal links and just a few external links with relevant keywords.

3. *Links or text is hidden in your content.* This is an old trick that used to work but now is a major "faux pas". Most of the time, this is used for malicious purposes; mainly to hide viruses and malware in posts or pages. While it could boost your posts and blog for a bit, it can run the risk of having your blog being banned from Google. It is really not worth the risk!

4. *Content is only test-focused.* Readers get bored with just words. They need a little visual stimulation. You can also add interest in call-outs and highlighted quotes to help break up the text. Doing this means readers stay longer, which helps your SEO.

5. *Each post has the same or a very similar heading.* While this can help boost your SEO, it will confuse and annoy your readers. This, in turn, will increase your bounce rate and hurt your SEO in the long run.

6. *Links to other websites are included with abandon and little research.* If Google has penalized a website for a certain

reason and you link to them, you could be unknowingly hurting yourself. In addition, if you link to a website with adult content, you could be damaging your blog and its SEO. If you do insert links to other sites or blogs, make sure you are doing so carefully and with a good understanding of the opportunity and risk.

Paid vs. Free Traffic

You can pay people to visit your site, or you can find ways to get them there for free. Both have their advantages, but both have their disadvantages too. Many successful, money-making bloggers choose to do a combination of the two, but the balance between paid and free is up to you. Paying for traffic means buying ads, mailing lists, etc. Anything that requires you to pay for it to reach or target an audience is considered a paid traffic generator. On the other hand, using resources, like social media's free resources, is a way to generate traffic without investing money. This does not necessarily make it "free", however, because the tradeoff is often a larger investment of time and energy. Below is a generic list of paid or free ideas to help drive more traffic to your blog:

1. Focus on developing and managing a quality mailing list.
2. Guest blog on other's sites to bring people back to your blog too.
3. Focus on improving your SEO as outlined in the previous section.
4. Come up with a plan to reach out to other bloggers to help you promote your content. They will probably do the same to you in the future. This is a win-win.
5. Follow other bloggers and post engaging and relevant comments on their posts.
6. Ask other bloggers to share your content, especially if you feature them in your post.
7. Create a post with a roundup of experts on a certain topic. Ask "experts" in a certain field or on a certain topic to offer their advice on a subject and tag them in the post.

8. Develop a list of valuable resources for your readers for a specific niche or topic.

9. Interview influential people and outline your discussion and takeaways from the conversation. Make sure to tag the person you interviewed and ask them to share the content with their followers too.

10. Run a contest.

11. Create a strategy for social media based on your analytics.

12. Always include social sharing buttons on your posts and your site.

13. Create and share infographics for your niche.

14. Creates slides to share on SlideShare for another reach.

15. Join relevant Facebook groups to your niche and post catchy and graphic-focused posts regularly.

16. Seek out opportunities to be interviewed or speak on podcasts.

17. Cover major events with your niche's perspective in mind.

18. Do not shy away from controversy. Be firm in an opinion, make a strong argument, and invite people to share their opinions and perspectives. Open a dialogue that is productive, not attacking. It is risky but "hot".

19. Stay transparent and clear while offering value to your readers.

20. Start a podcast related to your blog.

21. Advertise on sites like Reddit or Facebook or StumbleUpon.

22. Create a challenge for blogging or sponsor one.

23. Offer a giveaway.

24. Join your local HARO group. This is a site that connects "sources" or "stories" to local reporters. Reporters are always looking for people to interview and you can be just one of those experts they meet with. If they use your information or

words in a story, make sure to ask that they publish your blog link too.

25. Spend time working on your strategy for your site map, email and signature responses, and keyword research. Creating a plan or strategy for maximizing these things frees up your time to stay focused on delivering quality content that counts.

Socializing, Commenting, and Being Heard

It can be isolating when you first enter the world of blogging. You can feel like you are turning from a real person with a passion into this Internet being churning out words and images for deep space. Try not to lose yourself in this process. You are a human being with a need for social connection. Blogging is an excellent method for developing this connection with no geographic, economic, etc., boundaries. The more you get out from your blog and engage with others, the stronger you build your blogger friendships and connections, but you also strengthen your individuality as a blogger. This is personal business, so make sure you stay connected to this.

It may sound enticing and easy to add a quick, meaningless comment to another blogger's post with a link to your blog. In that context, yes it is, but if you want to be professional and not get tagged for spamming, you need to add value to the discussion with your post, as well as your backlink to your blog or specific blog post. For example, instead of saying something like, "Great topic! John Doe, **www.johndoeblog.com**," try adding a comment like, "Wow, I like your stance on sustainability in fashion. Very bold! How do you see large corporate companies embracing this concept over making money? I'm curious about how you would approach that conversation! Thanks for sharing. John Doe, **www.johndoeblogs.com**." This type of comment opens up the opportunity to connect and engage with the other blogger in a meaningful way. The first example offers no opportunity for connection or content.

Try to avoid adding comments for the sake of adding comments and stay away from things like,

- "Nice post!"
- "Amazing share!"
- "Great details!"

Instead of wasting your time on this meaningless commentary, try the following:

1. Use Gravatar to add an image to your profile used for commenting on blogs.

2. When you read another bloggers' posts, try to figure out how you can add value to their information.

3. If you liked the post enough to share it on your social media channels, let the blogger know in the comments section. This is a sign of respect and appreciation for a job well done.

Chapter 4: Monetizing Your Blog

Monetizing Your Blog Like A Pro

Making money from your blog, your voice, and your words are possible, but it is not simple. It is not an easy process, especially if you are looking to make money rather than just play around as a Hobbyist. The fact remains that online marketing is necessary for the success of your blog and your income. There are basics you need to know and follow in order for this to happen. The purpose of this chapter is to offer these basics to you in a way that is clear and foundational. This way you can use the information to grow and develop alongside your blog. It is truly the best way to monetize your blog as a professional blogger.

There are five "laws" you must obey for a successful blog. Following these laws will lead to long-term success. Ignoring them will make your life harder, and your blog will struggle to find the success you desire. The fives laws are:

1. Focus
2. Quality
3. Value
4. Engagement
5. Authority

First, you need a niche. You need to have a clear focus on your content and your audience. Do not try to be all things to everyone or spread your content out all over the place. Even Lifestyle bloggers have a series of topics that they regularly cover for their targeted niche. You want a "core" full of loyal and engaged readers. If you start veering off on topics that are not related to them, you start to lose their interest, and therefore, start to lose their loyalty. The best way to solve your audience's problems is to stay on topic.

Your topic needs to be valuable to your audience, not just to you. Value comes in the form of a well-researched and well-written piece of content that has sources, links, and in-depth knowledge. The more quality you offer in a single post, the better. Quality is always better than quantity in the world of blogging. This value teaches, instructs, guides, and delivers to your audience. Think tutorials, infographics, etc., designed just for your niche. People learn in different ways, so include different ways to reach people with the same message. For example, some people love and thrive by reading about something, while visuals are better for others. In addition, hearing content is another method people learn best. This means having text, images, and a short video in a single post can be a powerful tool to reach more people. You do not need to do this every time, but it is a good idea to remember this when developing your content and promo strategy.

When you create content that people value and you are obviously aiming to help your audience more than focus on yourself, you have a greater chance of engaging them. The more people engage and spend time on your content, the more money you can make. You can make this money by selling your products or through other monetization strategies. The fact is: the more people that spend more time on your content means the more you can make. They are not going to engage in your content that does not have focus, quality, or value, so make sure to check those boxes off first before trying to get people to interact with your posts. And when you have those first three things checked off, you also have a better chance at the fifth "law"; authority. If you are not already considered an expert or authority in your niche, your amazing posts will start developing that reputation for you. The stronger your reputation as a leader in this niche is, the better the opportunity for engaging an audience and making money you will have. This is called "leveraging" your influence, and there is nothing wrong with it as long as you keep the first three points in mind every time.

These "laws" were covered in the previous chapters; so hopefully, they are not "new news". But now that you understand the link between all of them and the importance of each, you can now focus on how to turn these laws into profits. There are generally eight different ways you can make money through blogging. Not all the methods are best for all types of blogs, but once you review the details of each, you can decide which ones to use for the niche you are targeting. Of course, there are always new and different methods for making money through your blog. As you read through this review of the "Core Eight", you may find yourself thinking, "Yeah, but what about..." The purpose of this is to introduce you to the major monetization methods that typically span across various types of blogs well. They are the "foundation" of money making through blogs. All the other ones that pop up are great, and maybe your bread-and-butter monetization in the future. However, for now, these are a great place to start:

1. Affiliate marketing

This is a big one. The biggest and most popular possibly. When you start out, this is one of the best things to leverage. Most likely, in the beginning, you do not have things to sell, so this method is great to start generating revenue. Just make sure that your content matches the affiliate promotion; for example, if you are writing about yoga, promoting affiliates links for yoga accessories like jewelry, home décor, and other accessories is a good avenue for your audience.

2. Advertisements (Ads)

PPC, or "Pay Per Click", is a popular method and something you can easily add to your blog; however, the income does not really start pouring in from this method until you reach between 10,000 and 100,000 visitors each day. This is a lot of expectations for a new blog and blogger. Instead, contact advertisers and seek to negotiate set terms for including their relevant advertisements on your blog. Remember: relevant. Most likely, doing this will bring you more money in the beginning than PPC ads would.

3. Market through email using your mailing list

Build your mailing list and send out regular emails. This is a powerful money-making method. You can use any one of the email marketing platforms out there to help you. While your email may not make money, the connection and loyalty you create will. People will be more likely to engage with your content and buy your products if you are connecting them to information that is valuable to them. A good estimate is to view each new mailing list subscriber as about $1 profit for you.

4. Sell eBooks, White Papers, etc.

Develop a book or an in-depth paper that digs in deeper regarding the content on your blog, and you can sell it to your readers looking for more. You can easily develop a non-fiction digital book that can teach and guide people more than just a simple post can do. Once you create your book, promote it on your blog and through social media. You can use this also to help generate leads and develop your mailing list. As you grow, look into a way to sell your book on autopilot, so it is a great form of passive income for you.

5. Sell workshops, courses, etc.

Like books, you can sell online training. If you can create training that is valuable and well researched, you can sell them for a decent amount of money. You should not think of your effort put into these as quick, done-in-an-hour-and-then-make-a-ton-of-money type courses. You need to put a lot of time and effort into creating an amazing workshop or course for your readers. Once you put in this effort, though, you should be able to sell them easily for a long time. Technical skills tend to work well as courses and workshops, but you can probably find a way to train someone on other topics like fitness, health, and fashion. A good goal is to find what is already being offered as a course in that niche and then come up with something even more valuable.

6. Sell digital products

You may not want or be able to set the time aside to write a book or record a stellar workshop or course right now. That does not mean that you cannot sell something valuable to your readers. Any digital item that is valuable to your readers can be sold for a profit. Think about a checklist or worksheet that your readers could benefit from. Digital content comes in many forms, including videos and PDFs. Find a gap in things your readers could use and put it out there. You will be surprised at the amount of money you can make offering a digital product like a checklist or training video.

7. Offer to coach your readers digitally

Just about everyone is offering to coach others in some form or another. While "everyone" is already doing it, you can profit from this too. You can coach people on healthy eating, living a good life, making money, succeeding in business, etc. Choose a topic you are knowledgeable about and can offer as a real service to your niche and develop a training program. You can make a significant chunk of money through just a few clients this way. Make sure when you do this that you cap the number of clients you are willing to take on at a time and answer questions or discuss concerns before getting started. Also, keep the transaction and interactions simple. The more complicated the process to sign up and get coached, the less likely you will have a steady stream of coaching clients.

8. Sponsorships

Like affiliate links and advertisements, this one relies on traffic. The more people you get to visit your blog, the more money you can make through sponsorships. Sponsored posts are great, but you need to be transparent about the sponsorship to your readers. You can get penalized if you are trying to pass off a sponsorship as "organic" and personally-driven content. It is not worth trying to hide the fact that you were paid or sponsored to write the review or post, so make it very clear what is going on in the post. Your readers will appreciate the transparency and Google will be accepting of your content.

Now that you are introduced to the different core methods for making money through your blog, it is time to dig a little bit deeper into each topic for you.

1. Affiliate Marketing

As a new blogger, affiliate marketing is a great way to start earning a little bit of money. There are several tips to help you get the most out of your efforts and to provide value to your readers better. First, choose just a handful of products or services to target. You can get carried away promoting, promoting, promoting, but your readers do not want to see a whole list of affiliate links and nothing of fresh perspective. The best bet is to choose a couple of things you are really passionate about and that you think can really help your readers, and aggressively promote those. This creates a cornerstone of your income through affiliate marketing. You can introduce other affiliate links that support blog topics or other content, even the main affiliate links you are promoting, but you need a couple that is your core.

Focusing on a handful of opportunity helps you focus on making money from them specifically. When you are thinking about your content for your next blog post, how can you integrate one or more of your cornerstone affiliates products or services? You can even use this to help design the layout of your next blog post. Even your email marketing can be influenced by the affiliate links. To get the most out of your affiliate marketing, make sure you can check off the majority of the following points:

- You have used the product or service in the past and know it is valuable personally.
- The product or service is very relevant to the majority of your niche, and it will interest most of them.
- The financial benefit of promoting this product or service is worth it. This does not mean it has to be a high payout, but that would be nice. It just needs to offer you something that makes promoting it worthwhile to you.

Once you choose your affiliate products or services, figure out where you are going to promote them. You only make money when a person clicks on the link and buys something. This means you need to put it where your niche will see it and take action. Great places to consider are on headers, in blog post content, listed at the end of a post, or even a section that leads into a post. Sidebars do not get much attention. Most readers ignore this spot because they know it is an advertisement. Instead, find a place that is obvious and prominent.

One of the most effective places to place an affiliate link is in an email. Your mailing list is a great place to start promoting your affiliations. Every email should not include a product or service promotion, but it can occasionally, and your email subscribers will be more likely to purchase something if they find your content valuable and trust your advice. You can develop trust through a valuable email marketing strategy and occasionally throw in an email with affiliate products in there. To succeed in this arena, constantly grow and enhance your email mailing list and marketing plan. Choosing an email marketing platform to help you maintain your mailing list and sending out customized content to your readers can also help you with having auto-responses set up to help promote your affiliate products. For example, no matter when a person subscribes, you can have a series of set emails that get out to them with content that you curate. One of more of those auto-response emails can include promotion of your affiliate links. For example, when a person subscribes, they get a series of ten introductory emails. Each one is spaced out to be sent a few days apart from one another, and the content is designed to be valuable and connected to their interests. The emails should have links to the products you are promoting and also back to your blog for more details. Once you set this up, the email marketing provider does all the work, bringing your mailing list back again and again to your blog with no more effort from you.

Hopefully, you have come to realize that just sticking a banner ad on the top of your blog is not going to cut it. Most affiliate programs offer banner ads for your site, and you should not completely discredit them, but they are not going to be how you generate the most sales from your affiliations. The reasons businesses are even offering affiliations are for a more organic appearance and personalized promotion of their products. Banner ads make it look like a paid advertisement, and this is not effective for you or them. Instead of relying only on banner ads, promote the products and services in different ways, like in blog content and email messages as mentioned earlier. Even publishing an entire post about the product and reviewing your experiences with it can be helpful. Make sure this review is honest and personal. Share the good and the bad in it. You can be honest that you receive monetary compensation for promoting the product or service, but that your review is your personal experience with the affiliation, and also, it is why you are promoting it in the first place.

If you write a review, or even if you do not, consider writing a post about how to use the product or service. Offer a tutorial with tips and suggestions on how to get the most out of it. Show readers how you integrate the affiliation in your personal life. This not only promotes the product but shows your readers how it can help them as it has helped you. Posting content in this way is a bit more organic and can also help in SEO. Consider adding posts like this to your auto-responder strategy so you can help your readers and generate affiliate income.

Also, make sure your evergreen posts have affiliate links in them somewhere or some way. You can also go back and add links to these key posts. If you add information to your older, high-performing posts, launch a new promotion strategy for them. Push the info back out through social media channels and link it in and to newer content that you have published. You can also guide people to these posts with the help of a "start here" landing page for new visitors. This homepage guides people to the top performing posts as well as content promoting your affiliate links. This is a great way to guide people right away to moneymakers for you and helpful content for them. When your readers find your promotions and affiliations valuable to them, you can ask them also to share your content with their network. This is essentially readers sharing your content to get you more exposure and money. Use resources like Social Locker, Just Retweet, and Viral Content Buzz to assist you.

Finally, do not be afraid to ask affiliate companies to give you more commission for promoting their content. If you are constantly promoting one or two different products and are generating a lot of sales for them, it is normal and acceptable to ask for a higher commission. It is common to receive a higher commission than what is advertised, especially if you have a track record of successful affiliate promotion. Companies pay more to keep top performers and also keep business away from their competition. When you ask for more commissions, have a strong case to justify the higher payout. This means being able to share your track record of success and how you are more effective than the average blogger with your strategy. You do not need to share details of your strategy, but you can show how your approach generates sales for the company, and this is what the whole purpose is for their affiliate program.

2. Ads

Contacting advertisers to have direct ads on your blog is a great and easy method for generating income. PPC is another method. Many bloggers rely on Google AdSense to help them make money through ads, but there are many other methods to consider and add to your blog in addition to Google AdSense. Below is a breakdown of different advertising methods to consider for your blog:

- *PPC*: Also called CPC or "Cost per Click". This just means that an advertiser will give you money for each click on the ad that they get from your blog. Advertisers like this include Infolinks, Media.net, and Chitika. Most of the time, you get your payout once you hit your minimum limits, such as $50 or $100, depending on the payout method you choose and the provider you choose to work with.

- *Sell ad space:* This is probably more financially beneficial for new blogs, but an advertiser needs to see that you are already bringing in a decent amount of traffic to make it worth it for them. If you offer ad space on your blog, develop a page for "Advertising with Us". This way, advertisers can go there to learn about how you plan to share their information and how much it costs them each month. This is also the place to share why it is valuable for them to pay to advertise with you. This includes rankings on Google, Alexa, etc. You can also use services for selling ad space on your blog too. For example, BuySellAds and BlogAds sell your ad space and take a percentage of the profits for their efforts. Most of the time, these companies will only work with established blogs with good traffic so make sure you get your page views and visitors up to use this type of service.

- *Offer text links for sale on your blog:* It is kind of like selling ad space, but be careful with this method. It is vital that you offer the "Nofollow" tag on the text link, so you do not get penalized from Google. Linkworth is a common provider for text links and offers a minimum payout between $25 and $100.

- *CPM:* Instead of being paid when a reader clicks on an ad, you are paid by the impressions. Instead of being paid with a click, when you have a certain number of visitors, you get paid a set amount. This means, for example, that you get $500 when 100,000 people see the ad. PulsePoint is a common option for CPM. It is important that you have a lot of original and fresh content often and decent traffic in order to capitalize on this option.

- *Pop-Ups:* Many people, bloggers, marketers, and readers alike do not like pop-ups. While they are not a popular option, it is still something you can consider. Thankfully, with many advertisers, you can choose how often you want the pop-up appearing on your site as well as your price. PopAds is a good option to consider for this type of advertisement.

- *Paid reviews:* This is not necessarily a traditional advertisement, but it is advertising a product for a company that you are paid to offer a review for. For example, if the company sends you a product to try out and write a piece for, you could receive anywhere between $150 and $500 as compensation. This does depend on your niche, traffic, and rank. Some companies will offer their own independent offers, or you can go through a resource like PayU2Blog or SponsoredReviews. The great thing about being paid to write reviews is that you do not need to write only positive content. The original, personal, and honest discussion of the products is what the companies are looking for through this method of advertising.

3. Selling digital products (eBooks, white papers, checklists, worksheets, etc.)

Digital products, also sometimes called "information products", refer to any type of digitally-based content that provides information and value to a customer. You can offer a video, eBook, audio recording, checklist, etc. A digital product is anything that has a tangible aspect. This means it does not include services like webinars, courses, coaching, and memberships. Those topics will be covered later in this chapter because they need a slightly different approach to making money and promotion.

This biggest difference between offering free content through your blog and selling digital content like a book or video is that you are offering more than just information; you are offering solutions and techniques to improve their lives. You are a guide and resource for their future advancement and growth. Your digital products need to bring that to them in more depth than your posts offer. You can offer other physical products, like a printed book, DVD, or other products, but for the interest of this section, the products discussed here are all digitally based. Those topics will be covered later in this chapter. The advantage of offering a digital product is that you do not need to pay and store inventory and then deal with shipping and delivery methods. Digital content offers immediate access for your customers and no major efforts on your part to store and distribute the content. If your reader orders your book at midnight on a Tuesday in Alabama and you are traveling in Europe for a few weeks, you do not have to figure out how to ship it to them—you can automate a message that sends the password to the gated content on your blog, and "poof!" they have instant access to your eBook right then. And for you, you do not have to worry about the added cost of all the physical products. Even though you can automate and sell digital products easily, you still have to worry about customer service and monitor sales though.

There are many advantages to selling digital "information products". Below are some of the major reasons to consider using this strategy to make money through your blog:

1. *Digital products are pretty easy to develop and are simple to design.* They are also inexpensive or even free to create. You may invest a little money into editing or adding a graphic design element to your products, but it is possible to

come up with something valuable and amazing without spending anything more than your mental energy and time to develop. The great added benefit with this is that, if the product does not sell like hotcakes, you are not out very much. This low risk is a great selling point for digital products.

2. *You do not have to pay for storage.* You can create it and store it on the Cloud, on your computer, and gated on your blog. No worry about inventory, inventory management, and storage for this method! And the illusion that you can just store physical inventory at your home is unrealistic and becomes very overwhelming and also limiting. Digital products do not require physical space, so take advantage!

So now that you know the value of offering these types of products through your blog, how do you create your valuable and relevant products? To start, you always want to begin with research. Determine what products are already selling for your niche. Your research can include visiting places like Amazon, eBay, online discussion boards, groups on social media, and major news sites. For digital products, make sure also to check Clickbank.com because they are focused primarily on digital products. It does offer information in other areas, but that is their primary niche. And once you get a good idea of what is and is not out there for your competition, you can also gather information about pricing as well. Keep in mind that you are not trying to be a pioneer here; you are looking to nudge your way into an already booming or blossoming trend for your niche. Being a pioneer is risky and often has more downsides to good. Instead, find a unique and personal voice to get into an already successful strategy. This means that there are a market and audience for this already—you just need to make sure that they see the value in what you have to offer.

Once you have an idea of what you want to offer and the price you want to charge for it, it is time to get down to actually creating it. For documents, develop them in Microsoft Word first and then save it as a PDF once you are done editing it. Make sure to get a professionally-designed cover for your document content. For example, hire a freelancer through Fiverr.com to come up with something nice to add to it. This can cost as little as $5, depending on the designer you choose and what your budget is. Even making a video can be little to no cost for you. Use your camera on your phone or point-and-shoot camera and then upload the video onto your computer. Use iMovie or Movie Maker, free software for most computer operating systems, to edit and refine the content. You can even add a nice audio file to it, making it look and sound more professional.

Creating an audio file is another interesting option for digital content. Just record your content through GarageBand or Sound Recorder and edit it when you are done. Make sure you have a good microphone for this type of content. For book writing, you do not need to be an expert in the written word to offer something informative and valuable to your readers. If you struggle with writing a book, consider hiring someone to do it for you. You can also interview professionals and record the interviews as a product. Another idea is to find digital products that are for sale and then rebrand the item to make it your own. There are many ways you can develop creative digital content and use it to make money, and you do not need to be an expert in creating this content format to be successful.

Once you get it created, you need to get it to your readers. Direct-response online marketing is a good way to push it out to millions of viewers, but it is not the most strategic or cost-effective. If you have the means to launch a big marketing push like this, give it a try. Otherwise, use your email mailing list to your advantage. Come up with a good and enticing email message and subject line to get your readers interested. From there, they can engage with your content, both free and paid for. The more you can mix free with paid information, the more you can generate interest and loyalty. Like traditional direct marketing campaigns, your email strategy will only result in a small number of people taking advantage of your digital products, but those small buyers should be bringing in a bit of profit. And once those people buy something from you, you can target them again in the future to buy more things like it. You can follow up the initial purchase with another option that offers more value at a higher price. Doing this "back end" selling is a great way to boost the sales you already have from the "front end", and often lower priced, products. For example, you can bring in people with a short white paper on a topic and then follow up that sale with an offer to buy an eBook that goes into more detail on the same or similar topic. Or you can offer a short how-to guide for the front-end sale and then access to a training video as a follow-up, back-end sale. In addition to your direct, email marketing strategy, make sure to write a blog post that leads to the promotion of your product and shares the information on social media.

4. Selling digital services (webinars, courses, memberships, coaching, etc.)

Services that you offer through your blog are anything that does not have a physical presence like a product. Services are unique to your niche and your voice. This is one of the best reasons to offer a service to your readers; you can offer something no one else can, and in a way no one can replicate. Sometimes, you can figure out what you will offer as a service through the comments and questions by your readers. If there is a common theme or problem your readers continue to struggle with, how can you help them through consultations, meetings, coaching, etc.? In addition to offering them the information they are seeking, a service can also give them the feeling of personalized attention. A blog post can offer general advice, but a coaching session can cut right to what they need or want. Below are a few ideas for services you can offer:

- *Blogging advice or assistance.* You are already a blogger, so when a business wants to start blogging, you are someone worth listening to and learning from. Most likely, you have done a lot of research (like reading this book!) and have learned from a few mistakes. Bringing this experience to a client can be incredibly valuable.

- *Social media service.* Like the blogging service listed above, you are already using social media to your profit and advantage for your blog. Your experience with growing your followers, increasing engagement, and building traffic can be used to help others. This is especially helpful for small business owners. Offer your expertise for a fee that slides based on how much help they need.

Of course, there are many other innovative service ideas you can develop that are more directly related to your blog content, and a few will be covered more in depth in other sections such as webinars and memberships. No matter what you decide to offer, always make sure it benefits your readers the most. If you offer something that is low cost but highly valuable, you can have more sales and increase your reputation, benefiting you for the long term.

Once you settle on the service you want to offer, you have to consider a few important things, such as how much time it is going to take to fulfill your offer and how you plan on gathering payment for your services. Your services are just one way for you to make money through your blog. This means that you still need to have time to dedicate to other activities, like writing for your blog! Make sure you have a set amount of time set aside for your services, and you do not thin yourself out in the process. Understanding how much you want to make from your services and how many hours you can invest in the process each month can also help you define how much you want to charge. For example, if you want to make $1,500 per month through online mentoring, and you want to give about 30 hours per month to this service, you need to charge about $50 per hour for the service. This breaks out to about seven or eight hours per week dedicated to mentoring clients. Now, look at the average cost of this service for competition in your niche and the reality of dedicating eight hours in the week to mentoring. If both are realistic, you are in a good spot.

In addition to understanding the amount of time you have to dedicate to your services and your income goals, you can figure out just how much you are going to make from your services. Ideally, the need is far greater than your availability, and you can start booking up spaces, filling future spots, ensuring revenue in the future and helping establish your reputation as a leader in the market. Make sure to have a place on your blog to highlight your services and talk about what you are offering. Make sure to show your readers why it is valuable to work with you or use your services. You should also include the cost of your services on this page. Promote this content through email mailings, social media, in posts, etc. Then make it really easy for people to pay you. Keep it simple and straightforward. Offer a "shopping cart" and accept PayPal. PayPal also offers a plug-in for most blog platforms and hosting sites that you can take advantage of.

Coaching

This is like mentoring. It means working with someone, typically one on one, to help them achieve a goal. You can also offer a group coaching session with a small group of people working towards the same goal. You can conduct these sessions over an online video calling service, like Skype, or you can communicate just through email or phone. It is wise to record the sessions for follow-up and additional coaching support. Sometimes, you can even edit this content to create additional products to sell on your blog! Just make sure that your coaching client gets a copy of the recording with tips from you that are valuable and "homework" they need to complete before the next session.

People seek coaches to get them to grow and bound forward in a certain area. Typically, the people searching for a coach are new to a certain thing or field. If you have been in or know a lot about a certain topic, most likely connected to the content of your blog, you can be a host of information for them. In addition, you can charge a high amount for your hourly services! One very important thing to keep in mind is that you need to make sure you are the right coach for the client. If your client is looking for answers that are more in depth or out of your range, do not try to fake it just to get their money. Let them know you are not the best fit for them and try to help them find someone else to help them. You will not only save your reputation, but you will also create a thankful, and possibly loyal, follower after that honest transaction.

Memberships

You have much to offer your readers. You are personal, sharing, and helpful. If your readers want more from you, offer it to them for a monthly fee. For example, readers who want more access to things you have to offer, consider signing them up for a gym-like membership to a special part of your blog. When they have a membership, offer them access to things like software, apps, templates, checklists, worksheets, recorded or live webinars, videos, how-to documents, reports, articles, etc. There are many reasons people choose to join a membership, but the main reasons are to make their life more simple or easy, to help them learn something faster, or get more details on information found online.

You should consider developing a membership site because of the many opportunities it offers you. One of the biggest ones is the steady income it offers. You know that you can count on their monthly membership fee each month as part of your revenue. If you are offering them valuable content that is refreshed often, you will retain your members month after month. Having a membership also helps boost your reputation as a leader in your niche. And the more your reputation spreads as a leader and expert, the more people that will sign up for your membership! It is a great spiral of success. In addition, it opens up more doors for selling services and products, like eBooks and coaching services. As you make your members happy with great content, you can count on them telling their friends, family, and co-workers about it too. This brings in more clients and readers, and these referrals are often the best leads for your business. If you want to encourage this type of word of mouth referral, consider offering an affiliate program to your members with a benefit to them for their referral that joins the membership program.

It may sound like a large time commitment and a lot of work to come up with a valuable membership site. Yes, it will take time from your week to make it great, but you can automate many things. Once you create content, you can create a strategy to engage your members without having to do a lot of new development or interaction. This then turns your membership into a very passive form of income that you can almost set it and forget it. After all, your membership site is online, so you can work on it or adjust things as needed from any place and at any time. All you need is a device with access to the Internet.

The challenge with running a membership site is that you do need to keep it fresh. Your clients need to have access to relevant and timely information in relation to your niche. And you almost always need to be recruiting members to your membership group so you can replace those that leave (some will leave no matter what you do or do not do. There are things outside of your control that influence people to quit memberships or cancel services) and build your income stream and reputation. In addition, while you can run a membership through email, most of the successful options offer them online. This means you will probably need to pay a bit more for these types of tools for your blog to function properly. And while it is possible to offer a quality membership as an automated service, you will still need to offer fresh content often. If you are charging a monthly fee for access to your most valuable information, make sure it is fresh often. In addition, consider offering a monthly webinar for members to discuss a certain topic in more detail, offer a free half hour of coaching, or give them early access to tools or tips that you have not yet released to the public.

Depending on your niche, your membership site may look different than others. For example, some membership sites are only for courses and webinar training. This is great for a niche that is technical or very complex. Another example of a membership site is one that offers reports, papers, and articles that are premium for the niche. Think of academic and scientific journals. These sites are memberships and require members to pay to access the entire content in their library. Another idea is to create a special community place to share ideas or discuss topics with like-minds, or a place to share trending news in a specific field. You can also offer digital content through your membership site instead of selling it individually. For example, if you have a lot of graphics, instead of selling rights to each one, you can have a membership set up so a client can access all your content for a set fee each month.

Honestly, just about any type of niche and any type of blogger can benefit from having a membership site as part of their blog. Even for hobbyists, creating a place for people to come and discuss topics or access information is invaluable in helping continue to offer value for the future. Memberships are valuable and can help in numerous ways. Think of what your niche and readers are already interested in, and figure out what you can do to make a membership beneficial to their life. Also, make sure you create the content for your membership site before you build and promote it. You want to give a great experience to your first few members, so spend time coming up with quality content for them, just like you would do if you have 1,000 members.

Once you launch your membership site, make sure it is active. Keep your content fresh and relevant. Work on recruiting new members often. Encourage a sense of community and a place for members to interact with one another. This is also a great place for you to engage with them. Reply to comments and questions promptly and be prepared to get more detailed, personal, or informative in these discussions than you would in a typical blog post. Your readers are paying for more of you, so make sure to give it to them here.

Webinars

Webinars are an amazing service you can give to your readers. You can offer live webinars or record content and sell it to them for anytime access. The purpose of the webinar is to bring resources and tips on a specific topic to one place. Then it is synthesized into a lesson format and presented to clients to help solve their problem or teach them something important to them. The information shared needs to be practical, useful, and applicable. The people who pay for your webinar should walk away with a new skill they can put into action. In addition to sharing knowledge, webinars are a great place to also promote your blog and other services or products for sale. Some of the best ways to make money through your webinars are by:

- *Dig into the topic and find as much relevant information as possible.* Keep it handy while presenting your information, even if you do not use all of it in the presentation. It is possible that you will get a question about it or that you will find it useful to interject additional content as you are presenting. This also shows your clients that you are an expert, know your stuff, and are well prepared. You show them that this presentation matters to you. The more fully developed and well prepared and edited your webinar is, the more success and profits you can expect.
- *Select your software carefully.* When you are preparing to host a webinar, you need to find a software program that makes sense for you and is good for your clients as well. In addition, you can choose a free option, or you can upgrade your webinar for a fee. Stick to your budget and what makes the most sense for your clients and yourself. ezTalks Webinar is an easy resource that does not cost a lot. It also is known for offering tools helpful in presenting a webinar in a user-friendly manner. Some of these helpful tools include whiteboard sharing, recording, surveys, polls, and reporting.
- *Share content on your webinar well.* If you are referring to links or other sites often throughout your presentation, offer those resources to your clients. You could even send the list

of resources being discussed to them before the actual event so that they can read ahead of time, but it also can instill a sense of confidence in their choice to pay for your webinar because you have clearly done a lot of research into what you are presenting to them. Another option is to sell your resource list as an add-on to your webinar. If you can give them access to a lot of additional content on the topic, they are likely willing to follow up your discussion with those resources you recommend and sell to them.

- *Promote outside and within.* Promote your webinar to the public through all the channels you can, including writing a blog teaser about it. And once you are presenting your webinar, include information and links to your other products, services, and blog. You can even offer a webinar to walk through another product you are selling. This way, if you sell the client that product, you can then follow up the sale with the webinar to help them get the most out of their purchase. Then your webinar can focus on some of the more nuanced features of your product and how they can get the most from it. This format further allows clients to talk with you in real time about their purchase and you can get fresh feedback that you can follow up on and ask more questions about, so you can better tailor your content and offerings for your readers and clients.

5. Selling physical products (Inventory and Dropshipping)

You do not need to just offer your readers access to digital content for solving their problems and answering their questions. You can come up with a physical product to offer them. You can create something one-of-a-kind and sell it or purchase a bit of inventory and offer it for sale. If you do not have the time, money or space to hold on to inventory, another option for selling physical inventory is dropshipping. Basically, this is when you list items for sale on your website but do not hold the inventory yourself. The manufacturer or another third-party seller holds on to the inventory until your reader places an order. Once they place an order with you, you turn around and place the order with the third-party. They are the ones that gather the product, package it, and ship it to your customer.

There are two ways you can determine pricing for dropshipped products. First, base your pricing on the quality and value of the item. If a product is more valuable to your readers, price it higher. Or, if you have two products for sale, price the lower quality one lower, and increase the price for the one of better quality. The second approach is determining the price based on what it costs you to sell it. For example, if you know that the sale of a certain item is going to cost you about $10, your price better is higher than $10. You can typically get drop shipped items at wholesale or very inexpensive, leaving a lot of room for profit.

It is not all easy and glorious, though. You do give up a lot of control by doing this. You cannot control who or when your supplier processes the order and ships the item to the customer. In addition, you cannot typically add your own branding materials to the package as a traditional retailer could. Also, quality could be unknown if you do not first purchase a test item from the supplier so you could be sending poor items to your customers, leading to negative reviews and increased customer service needs. You must decide if the products you want to offer to your readers are worth the sacrifices.

To add drop shipping to your blog, look for plug-ins like jigoshop, ecwild, or woocommerce. Another popular option is the AliDropship plug-in. Other platforms offer e-commerce such as shopify and oberlo. Before you get too far into this, check with your blog platform to see if they offer an e-commerce function already that you can use or see if they are optimized for one of these plug-ins. Keep in mind that the focus is on your blog and then on products, so do not get too caught up in making sure your blog can sell these products from it. You can always find a workaround if you cannot.

Chapter 5: Managing Your Multiple Passive Income Streams

Your Blog: Your New Business Platform

In order for you to have long-term success with your profitable blog, you need to think a bit like a businessperson. Again, as mentioned much earlier in this book, blogging is not a passive income stream. You can make passive income through your blog, but the act of blogging and building a successful blog is often a full-time job. It requires constant content creation, networking, and marketing. Most of the time, the biggest hurdle to your success is your perceptions. You may have come to blogging with the illusion that you will be raking in piles of money while hardly lifting a finger. Paid advertisements would grace the edges of a beautiful site while sponsors are begging you to try their products and offering large sums of cash to talk about them. This is not always the case, and when this does not happen, you may slip into the mindset that blogging, therefore, cannot make you money like "promised". This is not the best method of approaching your blogging business, because, after all, it is a business to make you income. It is time to make sure your mind is thinking like a business.

For starters, you came to blogging because you have a voice and you want to use that voice to talk about a certain niche. This may create the illusion that you can talk about whatever you want whenever you want because this is your platform to do so. This is a Hobbyist perspective. You are here to make money and share your opinion. This means you need to approach as more like an Entrepreneur. Like any good business, you need a plan for success. You need to think of strategy and growth. It needs to stop being about you and your whims and more about those that you want to reach. Yes, this can be complicated and hard. It takes time and attention, and often a learning curve. However, you came to blogging to write, not fret about data analytics! Well, if you are coming to blogging also to create an income, you need to delve a bit into this as well. The business of running a business is not that complicated. You need to simply offer a solution to the problem your niche is facing. If you can find a big enough problem, and can clearly share your solution to people, you are going to succeed. It is all the little details that can feel like the whole thing is bogging you down. If you ever feel like this, pull yourself back to this basic understanding and come at it again from a fresh approach. You will do great with this perspective.

It can also be hard to justify to yourself and others why you are spending money on a blog. It is especially hard to justify when the blog is not making you any money yet. Expecting a business to boom overnight is unrealistic. Sure, it has happened a time or two to a select few, but for the majority of business owners, it took years for their investment in their business to pay off. Blogging is a business if you want it to make you money. This means you need to "spend money to make money." No, you do not want to go spending thousands on random paid advertisements without training or strategy, but you do want to spend money on getting the skills and best tools in place to set up your opportunity for success.

A great advantage of online business like a blog is that you are not tied to a physical location, but sometimes, bloggers act like they are. They act like their audience has to come to their blog to read their content, and therefore, make money. The reality is: you can go to your readers too. You do not always have to make them come back to your website in order to have a successful blog. You can share the content straight through an email or valuable information only on Facebook. The idea is to establish yourself as a value giver. This is what creates loyalty and a strong following. This is what leads to long-term success and good revenue streams. You are not tied to your blog, waiting and wishing for someone to engage with it. Get it out there and mingle with the digital world!

If you sat holed up in your house all day you would also lose touch with what your friends, family, and clients are doing. You would not know what they really needed from you. You may even wonder what you could possibly offer them to help fulfill their needs. You need to get out and engage so that you can get an idea of what is really happening in your niche. You can also find pockets of people that have not heard your voice and solution yet. You have no geographic or other boundaries that traditional businesses struggle with, so take advantage of it. There is so much opportunity.

All this opportunity and business can feel exhausting. And in the beginning, it is hard, but as you get used to the process and work your plan, you will find a rhythm that is sustainable for you. In addition, you will probably and should be developing a network of other bloggers to help support and grow your blog. And in return, you should be helping and supporting theirs. Of course, you will want to choose your blogger network carefully, making sure it is a quality connection that encourages this growth mindset. Do not jump on the "hamster wheel" of meaningless comments and empty "views" just for the sake of fluffing up numbers. Look for content, quality, and value even in these connections, and you will create a sustainable and long-term blog that you are both proud of and profiting from. Change your mindset to that of a businessperson, and you can grow your blog-business effectively.

Not Just a Side-Hustle: Go Full-Time on Passive Income

Throughout this book, you have been exposed to tools, tips, and techniques for creating and running a successful, money-making blog. However, now that you know all of this information, it is time to set it in motion and make it happen. To begin, you need an objective. This is a description of how you will begin shifting your focus full time onto your blog while creating full-time income (hopefully!).

Here are some tips on how to help you get clear on what you want so you can move from "side hustle" to "full time":

1. *Get clear on what you want to do.* You will learn more about how to set a realistic and attainable goal in the next section of this chapter, but you should have an idea of the goal, even if the goal at this point is just to turn your "side hustle" into "full time". Keep this goal in mind as you go forward, so you stay on the path where you intend to go.

2. *Slow growth is still growth.* In fact, slow is good. Just because you made a little bit of money through your blog does not mean you are ready to let your full-time job go just yet. Instead, move slow, and make sure your blog is a sustainable income source. The first few months of juggling basically two full-time jobs is tough and exhausting. This is where a plan comes in handy, but recognize that this is not forever and you will have a break soon. Just keep plugging along as best you can until you can make the transition.

3. *Make friends and connections.* You need to get your name out there. You need to be noticed. This can be uncomfortable, but remember that this is for your business. This is not you personally posting about your dog, but rather sharing it to grow your income and support your life. In fact, starting out, be bold and tell people you are connected to on social media what you are working on and ask them for help! Get them on your side and invested in your success too! Just by putting it out there and being honest can grow your business by leaps and bounds.

4. *Pump up your followers in all areas.* Yes, you are writing a blog. But if you learned nothing from the previous chapters

about social media, you need to use it to your advantage. This means getting more and more people to follow you in different places so that you can lead them back time and time again to your blog posts. You do not need to shy away from asking them to follow you from one place to the other. Ask your Facebook friends to follow you on Pinterest and Instagram. When you move from a side gig to full-time hustle, you want to have some hype around it. Having a strong social presence is a great way to boost that news the minute you go big.

5. *Let the fear help you fly as you leap into a full-time blogger status.* You will be scared at some point. Fear will play a big or small role in your transition, but it will be there. You will also have self-doubt—if not others doubting you. You will probably think that stalling before you go full time is good. After all, the second tip on this list is to move slow. However, at some point, you will know you are ready to leap into this but are afraid to do it. To make sure you are ready, make sure to check off the following:

   a. You have set a clear and realistic plan to turn your side hustle blog into a full-time income.

   b. You are already making good money from your blog.

   c. Your blog and income are growing steadily over time.

   d. Your instincts are telling you that it is time, even if your head is telling you a "rational" reason not to.

What Next?

Now that you have these introductory tips and advice, you are ready to get going and give it a try! All this information can feel overwhelming (see comments on this in the first part of this chapter!), so the following are a few time management tips to help you get started with it all. Sometimes, it helps to look at a calendar for the rest of the year, imagine where you want to be by December, and start planning a posting strategy to get you there. Your goal can be financial or traffic-related or simply to be consistently blogging from now until then. Consistency is vital to your success, so focusing on this, especially in the beginning, can help keep you on track and motivated.

There is so much information on this topic, and always something more to learn as the online landscape continues to change and evolve. While you get started, remain a student of the process. Learn and read as much as you can to help you grow. The tips in this book are relevant to helping you get started right now, but in the future, new advancements, options, opportunities, and changes may shift the advice here and your approach out there. The important thing is that you get going and give it a try. Insert different strategies to bring in passive income through your blog, keep a finger on the pulse of your niche, and allow your personality and voice to ring strong in all the valuable content you produce.

Below are some tips to help you manage your time starting your profitable blog:

- Determine the goal for your blog and keep that goal posted where you can see it. Make sure you set "S.M.A.R.T." goals. This means goals that are "specific, measurable, attainable, relevant, and timely." An example of a "S.M.A.R.T." goal is below. The blank lines under the example are for you to try your hand at writing your own "S.M.A.R.T." goal:
    - Specific: Increase page views by 15%
    - Specific: _____
    _____

    - Measurable: Using Google Analytics to watch the fluctuations in views from current until reaching a 15% increase.
    - Measurable: _____
    _____
    _____

o Attainable: Page views will grow through an increased focus on lead generation, which includes a more aggressive posting schedule, guest blog strategy, and a challenge.

o Attainable: _____

_____

_____

_____

_____

_____

o Relevant: Increasing page views will elevate my blog's ability to get sponsorships and more income through affiliate links.

o Relevant: _____

_____

_____

o Timely: The increase will occur over the next nine months in response to the activities planned for that time frame.

o Timely: _____

_____

• Plan ahead for how you will succeed. This means looking at all the actions you need to do in a day and week and setting a specific amount of time to do it. Do not "hope" to fit it into your day at some point. Instead, carve out hours to dedicate to your blog's success. Consider the following actions and what days and times you will give to these activities:

o Research: _____

_____

o Writing: _____

_____

o Editing: _____

_____

o Comment response: _____

_____

o Promotion: _____

_____

o Review other blogs: _____

_____

o Comment on other blogs: _____

_____

- Keep a notebook on you at all times to track your ideas. This can be an electronic method for taking notes, or it can be a physical journal you carry around. Whatever you decide, just make sure you have a way to write down the brilliant thoughts that pop into your head or the cool observations you make throughout the day. This is especially helpful if blogging is not your full-time job. Setting time aside to brainstorm can be a challenge. You can also snap a picture of something interesting you see while out or ask to record an engaging conversation.

- Friends are the best people to start with when it comes to research. This means going to coffee with a few friends, or giving them a quick call, and asking their opinion about what you are researching. Write down their impressions of the topic. This can also help you redefine how you present the concept. For example, if you pose a question to them and they get confused about what you are asking, work out how to rephrase it, so they get it, and then use that rephrase to help in writing your content. Once you get their perspective, then add in some information you find online to round out the fresh approach.

- When you set time for work, do nothing but work. This means getting rid of anything can distract you. Turn off the TV, silence your phone, turn off notifications online, etc. The time you set for this is important and deserves your attention. Give it all you got for the time you set for it, and then get up and go back to handling life. The chances are that your world will not fall apart for an hour or two while you get work done. (Of course, if it is an emergency and the world is falling apart, go handle it and then reschedule the time for your blog later in the day or that week.)

- As you sit down to write your first blog post or your 400th, you need to approach it the same way: write. Do not worry about the editing bit that is scheduled for later. It is scheduled for a reason. This time you have for writing is meant for just that; writing. Do not fret over the introductory sentence or the flow from one paragraph to another. If staring at a blank page is intimidating, consider developing an outline and flushing it out from there. This helps to keep your points on target. While you are flowing, you will probably come up with just the right sentence to start or intro into the topic.

- Do not try to be everything to everyone, including to you. If you are terrible at editing photos or do not understand Photoshop, outsource it. If you are struggling with keeping up with your email blasts and editing, hire someone. You can get a virtual assistant that can take on a lot of the day-to-day tasks, or you can purchase quality images and video for a low price on sites like fiverr.com, elance.com, and freelancer.com. You only have 24 hours in a day, and there are many commitments you need to handle during that time. If you find you are struggling with getting it all done, look for ways to get help. It may cost you more than you like in the beginning, but when you are bringing in a good stream of income from your blog, it will be worth it.

- Use the automation and scheduler tools available. You can schedule just about everything from your social media posts to publishing a new blog. Consider scheduling assistants like Buffer, Everypost, and Hootsuite to help you. With a service like this, you no longer have to log into each social site individually to develop your posts, but just plan it out in one place, tell it when to make it public, and move on. If budget is your concern, try out TweetDeck for your Facebook and Twitter accounts, but be aware that it is limited.

- If you are struggling with coming up with fresh content still, reach out for a guest blog or reader perspectives on a topic. Maybe even once a week, offer a chance for your readers to be heard or other bloggers to chime in with their thoughts. This is an amazing way to engage your readers, connect other bloggers and their audience to your site, and strengthen your reputation in your niche.

- Read and follow other bloggers that are your direct and indirect competition. Yes, part of your job is to read interesting blogs! You are not doing this to copy and plagiarize what others are doing, but what you are doing is getting ideas of what is already being talked about and how it is presented and what is still left on the table about a certain topic. You can also refine your voice in your writing by seeing how others present their ideas to their audience. In addition, it allows you to connect with other bloggers in your niche and create meaningful partnerships and discussions that benefit you both.

Conclusion

Thank you for making it through to the end of *Blogging For Beginners: Proven Strategies for Marketing Your Blog in 2019 and Making a Profit with Your Writing by Creating Multiple Streams of Passive Income.* It should have been informative and provided you with all of the tools you need to achieve your goals, whatever they may be.

Now that you have learned about the basics, you are ready to start developing content, getting onto your blog, and making some money. Use the tools in this guide to choose the best platform and topics for your posts. Decide how you are going to generate income, possibly through a mix of affiliate links and digital content or e-commerce. Schedule your posts to go live and set up a social media marketing strategy to promote your content. Work on your strategy to develop your mailing list and lead generation, so you continue to bring people to your blog and begin establishing yourself as an expert in your niche.

Blogging takes a bit of time to establish yourself in your field, so put in the effort with the understanding that it will pay off in the long run as long as you stick to it. Remember why you are doing it by keeping your goal posted where you can see it often. And always keep your focus on your readers, not on yourself. Bring your passion to them, and it will not only benefit both parties, but you will be more successful for longer this way. The more you benefit your readers, the more you will make. It may sound simple, but it is easy to forget. If you find yourself slipping away from being customer focused, put up another note posted by the goal that brings you back to them. You will not regret it!

And if you find yourself continuing to slip, question, or wonder, remember you can always come back to this resource to help you build and grow. Of course, this is designed for the beginner in mind, but these foundational concepts are always good to reflect on as you grow. Sometimes, simple is the best! You are on the precipice of living a life of passion and purpose, being paid to contribute your voice to the world. Now is the time to spring forward, grab your future, and enjoy your success. You have the drive, the tools, and passion. Now all you need is the action! You are ready!

Finally, if you found this book useful in any way, a review on Amazon is always appreciated!

Made in the USA
Middletown, DE
05 September 2019